'I can't go to school!'

of related interest

My Anxiety Handbook
Getting Back on Track
Birdie Gallagher, Sue Knowles and Phoebe McEwan
Illustrated by Emmeline Pidgen
ISBN 978 1 78592 440 8
eISBN 978 1 78450 813 5

The Mentally Healthy Schools Workbook
Practical Tips, Ideas, Action Plans and Worksheets for Making Meaningful Change
Pooky Knightsmith
Foreword by Norman Lamb
ISBN 978 1 78775 148 4
eISBN 978 1 78775 149 1

The ACT Workbook for Teens with OCD
Unhook Yourself and Live Life to the Full
Patricia Zurita Ona
Illustrated by Louise Gardner
Foreword by Stuart Ralph
ISBN 978 1 78775 083 8
eISBN 978 1 78775 084 5

Riley the Brave Makes it to School
A Story with Tips and Tricks for Tough Transitions
Jessica Sinarski
Illustrated by Zachary Kline
ISBN 978 1 78775 518 5
eISBN 978 1 78775 519 2

'I can't go to school!'

The School Non-Attender's Workbook

Suzy Rowland

Illustrated by Adam A. Freeman

Jessica Kingsley Publishers
London and Philadelphia

First published in Great Britain in 2023 by Jessica Kingsley Publishers
An imprint of Hodder & Stoughton Ltd
An Hachette Company

3

A CIP catalogue record for this title is available from the
British Library and the Library of Congress

ISBN 978 1 83997 206 5
eISBN 978 1 83997 207 2

Printed and bound in Great Britain by Bell & Bain Limited

Jessica Kingsley Publishers' policy is to use papers that are natural, renewable and recyclable products and made from wood grown in sustainable forests. The logging and manufacturing processes are expected to conform to the environmental regulations of the country of origin.

Jessica Kingsley Publishers
Carmelite House
50 Victoria Embankment
London EC4Y 0DZ

www.jkp.com

MIX
Paper | Supporting responsible forestry
FSC® C007785

Contents

Introducing Your Workbook   7

1. How to Use This Workbook   9

2. You're Not in Trouble   19

3. You Want to Go to School But You Can't   29

4. Your Virtual Worry Basket and Worry Bin   33

5. How and Why Anxiety Shows Up in Your Body   45

6. Ever Been to a Place Called 'Dread'?   53

7. When Adults Make Demands   61

8. A Bit More about Stress and How to Manage It   73

9. When the Bullying and Peer Pressure Gets Too Much   79

10. Your Ideal School   87

11. Being Away from the People and Places that Make You Feel Safe   97

12. The Magic Question   101

13. The Word Wall   115

14. The Pleasures and Pains of Being YOU, Including Self-Care   119

Online Help and Resources   125

Blank for Notes   127

Introducing Your Workbook

Throughout this workbook you will hear stories from a group of young people I interviewed, aged between 12 and 19.[1] This is a personal message to all of you (and your parents) who helped me with my research. I enjoyed chatting to you all. Even though you were going through a tricky time, you were so kind to share your thoughts and experiences to help others who are going through a similar experience to you. You are all s/heroes.

In this book you will meet the following children and young people:

Freddie is 12 and Irish. He is good at drawing, likes animals, prefers to type rather than talk, has long hair over one eye, and lives in Ireland with his mum, dad and older sister. He doesn't have a diagnosis of anything, but shows signs of early trauma due to serious bullying at school.

Marchelle is 15, of Caribbean heritage and autistic. She is in Year 11, getting ready for her GCSEs. She lives with her mum, older sister, nephew and older brother, who is also autistic. Marchelle is softly spoken, and seems quite sad about her life right now.

Nadia is 19, white and was diagnosed as autistic as I was writing this workbook. She was just getting used to this diagnosis, although her parents had thought this for a few years.

---

1   To protect their anonymity, all names have been changed.

Joel is 15, white and lives in London. He was diagnosed with autism and attention-deficit hyperactivity disorder (ADHD) a year before I interviewed him, as well as having ARFID (avoidant/restrictive food intake disorder) and mental health issues. Although he declined to give any specific quotes, he was happy for his experiences to be reflected.

Pixie is 15 and Irish. She was diagnosed as autistic when she was 13, and is totally cool about it. She is super-clever and confident, and great with younger kids. She could be a teacher one day!

Samila is 17, of Asian heritage, and living in London. She has an autism diagnosis and is on the road to an ADHD diagnosis. She has a mega-fast brain and speaks quickly and for a long time when I ask her any questions. Oh, and she has dyed her hair blue, which suits her. She figures she already stands out anyway.

How to Use This Workbook

You've probably been given this workbook to read by an adult who cares about you and is worried about you. Perhaps you're with a teacher, parent,[1] support worker or SENCO (special educational needs coordinator). All of your adult helpers who are reading the workbook with you can get FREE downloadable guides just for them using the following code SSFXXWY at https://library.jkp.com/redeem. Here, they will find a guide for professionals (such as teachers and speech and language therapists), and there is also a free guide for parents.

If you're a teacher, parent, support worker, SENDCO (special educational needs and/or disabilities coordinator)[2] or other professional reading this with a young person in your care, it's great to have you here. Working together will give you the SUCCESS FACTOR! And please download the parents' guide and perhaps go through that with your young person too, if this is helpful.

If you're a young person who isn't going to school, you probably don't feel like talking to anyone. Your thoughts may feel muddled, especially when someone asks you what you want or what you are worried about. If you find it hard to explain your thoughts in a way that people will understand, this workbook will help you to figure out how you got here, and what you can do next. If someone close to you is hurting you, either an adult or another child, skip straight to 'Online

---

1   Where I refer to 'parent', I mean both parents and carers.
2   Some schools and professionals use SENCO and others SENDCO. For consistency I will use SENCO, but I reassure you that this role includes coordinating the educational needs of children with all disabilities.

Help and Resources' at the end of the book (see page 125) for places to find help, such as the Samaritans or NSPCC.

You will see a picture of a little trumpet at the end of each chapter. This is to remind you that you *are* making progress, and that you need to celebrate your success!

Getting started

As you hold this workbook in your hand right now, remember – even though you feel stressed out and sad – there is always someone looking out for you and taking care of you or someone who wants to help. Sometimes the adults around you will get things wrong and upset you, but they are still trying to help and they do care. Later in this workbook I will share a few techniques to help you tell the adults around you what you want and what you don't want. Sometimes, adults find it hard to listen to children and young people, but there are ways to make it easier for them to listen (jump to Chapter 2, page 23, and the ABC technique now).

I've talked to lots of young people aged from 11 to 19 while doing research for this workbook. Their stories are different, but they all have one thing in common – they are in distress and need help to get 'unstuck'. Help is available, but it can be hard to take the first step. Talking to strangers can also be hard. I hope this workbook encourages you to take that first step. The young people I spoke to are clever, funny, creative and kind. I bet you are like that too. But many are also full of worries, and don't have many friends. They worry about not saying the right thing or fitting in. Others worry about climate change, the future, crime, drugs and a world of other things that are just too sad to think about. Do you share some of their concerns?

Your rain cloud full of worries

There are many reasons why you might be off school right now. A whole rain cloud of things could be bothering you. Can you see any of your troubles in this heavy rain cloud?

If you feel you can, tell a trusted adult which of the issues in the rain cloud relate to you.

I will let you into a secret...rain clouds don't stick around forever. The rain comes down to refresh the earth and the sun comes out – if you're really lucky, you will even see a rainbow...

Your rainbows full of joy

These are some of the feelings you will experience in the rainbow – and this is what you have to look forward to!

I will let you into another secret – rainbows fade. Somewhere between the rain clouds and the sunshine is everyday life. When things feel boring and routine and same-y, that's okay. Things go wrong, people upset you, they annoy you and make you sad, and that's okay too – because life is all of this...rainbows, sunshine, rain clouds and shades of grey, all random. Even though it would be better if we didn't have the rain clouds or the shades of grey, we all do. This workbook will give you some ideas to manage in the grey or rainy times when they come. And how to enjoy the sunny rainbow times too!

We are all unique

This workbook is for you and about you. You are a child or a young person, but most importantly of all, you are an *individual*, with your own thoughts and needs. When I was a little girl, I felt wise and grown up. I grew up with just my mum and me – my parents were divorced and I was an only child. I knew what I wanted to do with my life: to communicate, heal and create using my writing skills. I meet lots of young people who know what they want to do with their lives, but sometimes things get in the way.

In some parts of the world, you are expected to go to school every day until you are at least 16. In some countries, children start school aged four. In others they start at seven or eight. That's quite a few years difference, isn't it? Can you remember when you first started school when you were little? Can you remember anything about the teachers and the other children? Or the lessons and playtime? How do these memories make you feel? Take a few moments to think about your early school days – write about them or draw some of your key memories, if you want to.

School is a privilege, for some

Going to school every day is – believe it or not – a luxury! In poorer parts of the world, many children can't go to school every day, because they haven't got shoes to walk there, or their parents haven't got the money to pay for schoolbooks, pencils, paper and a uniform, or they need to help their parents on a farm or in a shop, or school is just too far to walk to. Some can't go to school because they have a disability and can't get there without help.

In richer countries, in the Victorian age, for example, getting an education was a privilege, just for the children of wealthy families! Some of these children had a governess (a fancy name for a woman who was employed by the family to teach the girls – it was usually girls – a variety of skills such as reading, playing the piano or sewing). Boys were also taught at home until they could attend a public school (aged about 10), when they would learn subjects like Latin and algebra as well as competitive sports.

We would be shocked if teachers were allowed to hit children across the hand or the back of the legs with a cane at school today, but this did used to happen! I am mentioning this because looking back at the past helps us to learn what we can do better for the future. Thankfully, education is much kinder to children today. Change can be positive, and create more kindness and understanding.

Getting an education is a privilege for many children growing up in countries where there isn't a free (state) education system, and it's only in the last few hundred years that getting an education has become more open to every child and adult. Some countries have enough wealth to pay for a free education for all children up to the age of 18. Poorer countries are not able to do this, which means they either don't go to school at all, go to school occasionally, or their parents have to pay lots of money for them to be able to go to school every day.

Every child is offered a school place

Over the years, governments have made laws stating that children should all get the same education, going to the same building every day, with 30 other children in a class, doing the same lessons each week, with children the same age as you, whether you like them or not! Teachers are given authority over you, and the choice of information you learn about is decided by the government of the day.

From the age of four or five you go to school every day. You keep going to school, sitting lots of tests (e.g., SATS – standardized assessment tests) and exams until you get to age 11 or 12. Then you go to another school (usually much bigger than your first one) until you are 16, when you sit more formal exams (in the UK they are called 'GCSEs'), and then you choose a smaller number of topics to study until you are 18. At 18, many sit 'A'-level exams, or Advanced Placement tests. Some re-take GCSEs to get better grades and others leave school to look for a job.

It may feel like your whole life, from the age of four or five until you are 18, is a long period of learning until you are an adult. Which is pretty accurate. Childhood and adolescence sometimes feels like you jumped on to a fast-moving conveyor belt as a cute four- or five-year-old, being fed lots and lots of information, and then you are spat out at the other end as an 18-year-old shaped sausage!

This may sound like an exaggeration, but consider how fast technology is changing around us. We are changing fast, becoming the unique beings we want to be, but the *fast, fast, faster* the conveyor belt whizzes along, some of you are left dazed, confused and unhappy, not getting it, not fitting in, getting told off. The speeding conveyor belt of schooling means that some of you experience growing up like being on a rollercoaster. Not enough time to catch your breath before you go on the next ride...

Do you ever feel like you want to stop?

The speed of growing up makes you feel a bit lost. There's not enough time to get used to the speed of the conveyor belt. You notice that your friends seem to pick up things faster than you. Your family is different. You have seen things that make you feel sad, every day.

Sometimes you want to get off this speeding conveyor belt, and take time to think about things. Talk to the sky. Write in your journal. Make up silly jokes. Have a lie-in on a Wednesday afternoon. Go and see a film when the cinema is more likely to be empty. Walk in the park with your mum and sister, without having to see the same people you see at school all day.

Imagine it's Tuesday afternoon (it might actually be!). This is your chance to get off that speeding conveyor belt. Take a minute to think about things. Flick through this workbook and see what catches your eye. Try some of the exercises.

How this workbook will help you

If your plan for going to school, staying at the same school, doing subjects you don't like, sounds tough, you're not wrong. And it's not just the subject lessons that can be tough; it can be the people too. Or your feelings when you think about going to school. Or the thoughts in your head. This workbook is going to help you unravel some of the stuff that is bothering you, to think more clearly and share your inner thoughts with the people who can help you.

Here are four ways this workbook will help:

- ✧ We will look at some of the *reasons why going to school is tricky for you* – and start to create a plan together.
- ✧ We will look at some of the *words you can use to get help* – creating a plan together.
- ✧ We will look at some techniques that will make *being at school feel better* for you.
- ✧ We will look at *other options* in case returning to school full-time is out of the question.

We will use the exercises in this workbook to help us create a plan together. This plan will be special – it will be individualized, based around what you need. It will be a plan that you can share with your trusted adults.

Remember at the beginning of the workbook that I said there are some adults who want to help you and who care about you? Well, can you count me in that group, please? I want to share a secret with you. Your problems might be big and ugly, but whatever they are, I will show you some science-based ideas to help you tackle them AND start to overcome them so you can move forward. Does this sound good? Take a deep breath and dive in – you're at the start of something really good.

Blow your trumpet for getting this far! Let's go!

You're Not in Trouble

WHY TEACHERS AND PARENTS WORRY
WHEN YOU MISS SCHOOL

You're not in trouble – although it might feel like that at first...

As Pixie explained:

> I tried earplugs; they made the noise in the classroom less intense, but they were quite uncomfortable, so I didn't wear those much. By the time we got to that stage, I already had such a strong association of the noise in the classroom and the emotions of anxiety, that even if everyone went dead silent, I probably would have had a hard time getting into the classroom. I was also getting an autism diagnosis at this time and I'm not sure the school knew how to deal with me, because I'm not a stereotypical autistic person: I mean, I'm not a boy, I don't play with trains! But I was obsessed with Harry Potter.

There are three main reasons why the adults in your life are keen for you to go to school:

- ◇ So that you can get an education – skills and qualifications will help you build your adult life
- ◇ To keep you safe – they will know where you are
- ◇ To look after your mental health – being home alone can make you sad.

Being left alone is fine. For a bit. But being left alone *for a long time* won't help you to feel better. Being alone with your thoughts can make you feel much worse. You might feel like your thoughts are taking over and you can't see what's real anymore. If you are alone and living in your head, it can be hard for anyone to help you.

A listening ear

If you need space to think and to figure things out, be alone. But don't be alone *all of the time*. Talking to your friends online or on your phone is a good thing to do. Talking to someone face to face is also really helpful if you feel rubbish and unable to get to school every day.

I get it, I really do – sometimes other people can be part of the problem, so try to think about just one or two people who make you feel happy and calm – people you trust. And spend some of your time with them, however you want to.

Try not to let your alone time grow into lonely time. Human beings are social animals, which means that we need other human beings to feel happy, and that to be healthy, we need to belong to a community of people. You may already feel isolated and have few friends or struggle to make friends. Working through the exercises in this workbook will help to build your confidence, which, in turn, will build your skills in talking to and making friends.

If an adult is asked about why you're not going to school, and you want to tell them your real feelings but don't think that they will listen, it can seem easier not to talk at all. Which is annoying, isn't it? They've spent years telling you to act like a 'big boy' or a 'big girl' and to do 'grown-up' things, and now that you are doing what you want and staying away from school, they keep telling you that you're 'a child' and 'should do what you're told'.

Adults can be so confusing. They want you to behave like an adult but then they treat you like a child. It's difficult because they want you to listen to them, but they don't always seem to listen to you. This is why you want to shut down and don't want to talk to or listen to anyone. You just want to be left alone.

Sometimes there are so many things that bug you...

But there are just as many things that will make you happy!

What's in your rain cloud? Remember we talked about some of the things that make you want to skip school? Not everyone at school is welcoming or friendly. Some of the other children are loud, naughty and mean. Even some of the teachers can be angry or scary, which can make going to school really hard. And there are mean kids and scary teachers at every school, not just yours.

If you jump to Chapter 10 there's a fun exercise where you can create your own imaginary school with your own rules, the sort of school you would jump out of bed to get to each morning! There are only two rules to play this game:

1. You need to use *loads of details* about your imaginary school.
2. You need to *share your ideas* with your trusted adult.

You know we talked earlier about adults not listening or saying things that are confusing or that you don't understand? This is because some adults have lost the skill of listening, *really listening*, to young people. You can't solve all of the problems adults have to deal with, but one of the important things you can do is help them to listen to you, especially if you're in distress. In the next few pages are some suggestions to build your confidence, which may also encourage adults to listen to you better!

What's happening right now at school?

Let's focus on your current school for a bit longer, and why you find it difficult to go there. The experience of school is different for everyone. Some of you will have had a lovely time in your first school, with lots of happy memories. Some of you will feel upset about children or even teachers who made you feel sad or perhaps stupid. It's natural to take some of your happy or sad memories with you and make comparisons between your old school and the new school.

People do this after any major life change. This is why the first year in high school/secondary school can create major upset for lots of kids/young people as they miss their old school friends and sometime their old teachers. It's normal to feel a sense of loss and sadness after any major life change, such as moving to a new house, having a new baby in the family or moving to a new town or city. Changing schools creates the same feelings.

Whatever your experience was, whatever school you're in now, it's clear that you've hit some problems. And the problems are BIG. They seem so BIG that you can hardly get your head around them. Here's something you can try to help you move on from being 'stuck' in your feelings, especially if you keep thinking about how things used to be.

Use this 'ABC' if you feel sad for what's gone before and unsure about what's coming next:

- ◇ **A**ffirmations
- ◇ **B**reathwork
- ◇ **C**onversation.

Affirmations

Affirmations are a great way to retrain your brain to think thoughts that are more comfortable. If your brain doesn't believe those thoughts at first, or they sound silly to you, the trick for this is in the repeating of these words. If you REPEAT the affirmations regularly OUT LOUD, your brain will believe the words, and they will seep into your subconscious mind (the same part of your brain that remembers song lyrics without trying).

Here are a few affirmations to get you started, but you can make up your own or with your trusted adult. Do try to keep them as short as possible:

I enjoyed what went before, and I believe that what is coming will be enjoyable for me too.

Things are always working out for me.

All of these uncomfortable feelings are fading away – I am feeling better already!

Breathwork

This is what it sounds like – working with your breath to shift your mood. Breathing is something we all do, without thinking. When you work with breath, you do deliberate exercises that have been proven to calm you down and stop your mind from racing.

Here are two ideas you can try:

- ✧ Box breathing: breathe in and out to the count of four while imagining that you are building a box in your head. Each 'in' breath is one side of the box and each 'out' breath is another side of the box, until you have completed the box, and then you start again. It's fun.
- ✧ 4-5-7 breath: breathe in for four counts (from your belly), hold your breath for five counts and breathe out or exhale for seven counts. This can be hard at first, so try to imagine on that long breath that you are breathing out all of your stress and worries. It feels like such a relief to feel the stress leaving your body. PHEW!

Get comfortable and sit with your eyes closed for 10 minutes and try the 4-5-7 breath until the feeling of sadness or worry starts to fade. This is how it works:

1. Breathe in for four counts: 1, 2, 3, 4.
2. Hold for five counts: 1, 2, 3, 4, 5.
3. Breathe out slowly for seven: 1, 2, 3, 4, 5, 6, 7.
4. Relax for a moment.
5. Start again.

Have a go at box breathing or the 4-5-7 breath when you feel stressed or overwhelmed.

Good work!

Conversation

Mmm, talking to other people… This is an issue for lots of the young people I meet. It might be the same for you, too, if you're autistic or struggle with confidence. It can be hard to know how to start a conversation and keep it going. And when you're in distress, it can be very hard. It's okay if you can't use words when you're feeling upset; perhaps you can tell your parent, therapist or other trusted adult how you like to communicate. You can use a communication device, draw pictures – whatever is comfortable for you.

Here are some conversation starters. The good thing about using them is that they get much easier the more you use them:

I would like to talk to you about something – is now a good time to talk?

Something is bothering me that I'd like to talk about.

I've been thinking about something and I'd like to speak to you about it…

My suggestion is that you practise saying these sentences in a clear voice and think about what your next sentence will be. These openers will give you the opportunity to be heard, and that's where you will be able to start to explain some of your feelings. Having conversations with adults can be especially hard, but please don't let that put you off.

Close your eyes and see if you can remember what the three 'ABC' techniques are that you can use. When you're ready, try the ABC exercises – **A**ffirmations, **B**reathwork – and after a while you may even feel like having a **C**onversation. You may not get on with either of your parents, you may live with your grandma, foster family or an aunt, or flit between mum and dad and their different families. Perhaps you don't feel you can really talk to any of the people around you because they are busy. That's okay. What about other people around you, people who are friends, or a friend's parents or a special teacher?

There are hundreds of reasons why you may want to be alone with your worries, but guess what? There are hundreds of ways to help you understand and tackle your worries, *if you talk to someone first.*

Five-minute break thing (you can ask for help if you need to!)

As you go through this workbook, I suggest you take five minutes at the end of each chapter to absorb the information you have read and think about it. There are exercises and things to do, so you could take five minutes to do the following: get a drink and a snack, make sure you have a piece of paper and something to write with, get comfortable, and then have a go at writing down some of your thoughts and feelings as we go along. Are you ready? And you can write in this workbook, too – that's why we've left you lots of space and places to write or doodle.

Write down the names of three people to talk to whom you trust:

. . . .

. . . .

. . . .

. . . .

Put those names in order of how much you like them or they make you feel comfortable.

Write their phone numbers and emails next to their names. (You can get people's emails and phone numbers by asking them directly or asking an adult who knows them. However, the law states that we need permission to have someone else's data, so for some people you will need to have permission from them before you can email them.)

Write them a little note (or draft a text or email) saying something along the lines of: 'Hi – I hope you don't mind. I would like to talk to you about something that's bothering me. Please message me back when you get this. Thank you, from [put your name].' Send them this note when you feel ready.

Once you've practiced your ABC exercise and worked out what's bothering you and who you want to talk to, you're almost ready to talk to your school teachers or helpers to see how they could support you at school. There are lots of adjustments that teachers can make to improve your experience of school, and it's worth trying different things, as you won't know what works until you try it!

You Want to Go to School But You Can't

SCHOOL ISN'T WORKING OUT FOR YOU!

The guilt trap

There are many difficult things about not going to school. Your teachers might be really kind, and your parent might be trying all sorts of rewards to encourage you to go. But if your feelings are too strong, making going to school (nearly) impossible, and you don't want to let anyone down, you might also be experiencing *guilt* about how it all makes you feel. Especially when your parents are receiving scary letters from your school or are even being asked to pay a fine.

There are two reasons why the school may be writing to your parents:

- ✧ Schools have a legal duty to ensure all children of school age attend school (1996 UK Education Act).
- ✧ Schools have a duty and responsibility to make sure that you are safe from harm.

If your attendance level is very low – you haven't been going to school for several weeks or you go in for a few days and are off again for the next few weeks – schools are legally required to step in. How they do so depends on the school and the headteacher, but they will usually gather a team of expert professionals (mental health support worker, educational psychologist, clinical psychologist, etc.) to work with you and your family to help you to return to school and continue your education.

If going back to school is out of the question for you, your school or other people connected to your school can also advise your parents on the rules about home educating you.

None of this is personal. You haven't done anything wrong. It's just that if your attendance drops below a certain level – usually 90% – this triggers a series of actions from school, for all young people.

While you are facing an issue that is unique and personal to you that makes it difficult for you to go to school, I will let you into a secret. Other people your age are going through something very similar to you. You don't know who they are, but they are indoors, too, not going to school. Struggling with family stuff. Friendship stuff. Health stuff. Body image stuff. Bullying stuff…you get the picture. Remember that *you are not alone*. And lots of other people are good at faking it, pretending to be okay when they're really not, not knowing who to turn to for help.

This is another reason why answering those letters from school is a good idea. There is usually someone the school knows who is *really good* at helping you sort out these complicated feelings. And they will keep all of your information secret, unless they think that you may be harmed if they don't share it with someone.

Adults can be really good at helping, especially if they're not part of your family. Sometimes it's easier to talk to someone who isn't in your family – maybe your family is linked to your stress and part of the reason why you can't go to school more regularly?

WHY GOING TO SCHOOL MIGHT BE HARD FOR YOU

(If you don't see your reason listed here, write it in a notebook or on a piece of paper you can keep with this workbook.)

Fear of failure * Exam pressure * Friendship problems * Personal problems * Health issues * Weight worries (need to lose weight or get stronger and fitter) * Body image * Comparing yourself with others * Not keeping up with schoolwork * Fear of illness * Worries about family * Crowded * Too noisy * *Too smelly * Too bright * Flooding your senses * Overwhelm * Can't remember things *

The number of things you can worry about is almost endless!

You might find yourself saying, 'I'm dreading my exams' or 'I'm dreading doing the class assembly'...these are all real reasons to feel fear or clam up and get butterflies in your stomach. But if the feeling is severe and you feel you can't go into school, or you can't leave your bedroom because the feelings are too overwhelming, it's worth sharing these thoughts with an adult. Maybe even use a simple scale to express the intensity of your feeling: 'If 5 is the worst I have ever felt, I can't even cry, I'm frozen with this feeling, I'm at a 5 out of 5.' Then hopefully an adult will recognize your distress and seek professional help for you.

Pixie shares her story:

It was the boys who were causing trouble in Year 6; they were giving my teacher a hard time, there was sexism in the classroom. They didn't realize the impact they were having on people like me, not being able to attend. There is a responsibility on society to ensure boys just don't get away with everything.

My entire education I was a buffer for the boys – my teachers would sit me in-between the most disruptive boys because I was meant to be a good influence. But those teachers were just sacrificing my education. The boys were rude, loud, mean, they teased me, and impacted my enjoyment of school. The focus should be on getting boys to behave better; they shouldn't be using a 10-year-old girl as a shield.

Trauma effects

The feeling of severe shock can stay in your body for weeks, months, even years after the event has passed. Experiencing a traumatic event in your life, such as parents' divorce, a new baby, the death of someone close, can trigger deep emotions that get 'stuck' in your body. Sometimes the intensity of the shock is difficult to get rid of, so the cells in your body 'remember' the trauma and wait for it to happen again, with your brain playing it over and over. This is distressing for you to experience, especially as it's so hard to talk about. I understand you might not know how to tell someone trusted, but starting a conversation with the words: 'I want to tell you something but it's difficult for me...' is a good place to start. Practice these words out loud.

Talking to someone won't fix everything but it will make the problem feel less heavy, and that's going to make you feel a lot better.

Although we think of 'worry' or anxiety as emotional feelings that happen in our head, they are also *physical feelings* that we experience as they travel through our bodies. You know that fuzzy feeling of excitement when you're looking forward to something? It's the same with strong negative emotions, too – they can make you feel like your stomach is rolling around, like you're being tossed about in a boat, or like the ground underneath your feet is moving like an earthquake. Pretty horrible, eh?

We've discussed lots of issues in this workbook and some of them will relate to you exactly. This is because psychologists have studied child and teen behaviour, and know what sorts of experiences can be particularly difficult. The good news is that if you share your worries with the people who are working with you on a back-to-school plan or supporting you with therapy, they can start to make the plan <u>personal</u> to you, which means you are more likely to feel happier at the end of this process.

YAY and SMILES to that!

Your Virtual Worry Basket and Worry Bin

WHAT TO DO WITH THE THOUGHTS THAT ARE BOTHERING YOU

You'll enjoy this chapter if you're an *over-thinker*. You'll really love this chapter if you're a *nail-biter*. You'll love these pages if you *lie awake worrying about stuff*. This chapter is for you if you think that things are always going wrong for you.

Can you imagine if you had a real-life worry basket? A little wicker basket or a cool back pack with all of your problems and worries piled in it? Instead of filling it with groceries and nice things to eat, you would fill it with things *you don't want*! It's also expandable, which means it can fit EVERYTHING in it, so you don't have to worry about having too many worries – it will hold all of them. And yes, adults have worries too, and you may feel bad about giving them yours, but the thing about worries is that once we share them around – like cake – they just get smaller and smaller. ☺

Imagine dragging the contents of your mind around in one of those old-fashioned patterned trollies that people take to the market with them? Do you think your worries are worse, better or the same as other people's? How do you know? Would you swap your problems with someone else's?

. . . .

. . . .

Having a worry basket that other people can't see is a pretty good idea. Here's what you'll need:

◇ A laptop or computer you have access to, so you can create a document on it. Give your document a file name, something like 'elliesprivateworrybasket.docx'.

◇ A clean shoebox and a piece of coloured paper to write your name on. Give it a title, something like 'Things I worry about – KEEP OUT!' Stick the coloured paper on the top of the shoebox with glue or tape. (Use glue, glitter, stickers or anything that makes it feel more like YOURS to decorate it.)

Here's what to do for your worry bin:

1. Find or borrow a small, clean wastepaper bin and put a plastic bag inside it.

2. Get some lined paper and write down the name of your worry, for example: school. Then draw an arrow from this like a

spider diagram, listing all of your worries about school such as 'making friends', 'bullying', 'teacher doesn't like me', or whatever your school worries are.

3. Talk through all of your small worries with your trusted adult one by one. This may take a few goes if this is difficult for you. You may notice talking about the smaller worries makes the BIG WORRY feel less big?

Now it's time to *check out* your worries...

Tick, underline or circle the worries from the list below that relate to you:

- ✧ Children are mean to me because of my racial difference.
- ✧ I can't concentrate at school.
- ✧ I don't have many friends.
- ✧ I don't like being away from people who are special to me (in case something happens to them).
- ✧ I don't like the journey to school because...
- ✧ I don't understand the schoolwork – I feel stupid.
- ✧ I feel extreme nervousness around other people.
- ✧ I misuse drugs and alcohol.
- ✧ I think I'm gay/bisexual.
- ✧ I think I'm trans/non-binary.
- ✧ I worry about everything; I'm a worrier.
- ✧ I'm autistic (or I have a diagnosis, or I'm waiting for an assessment).
- ✧ I'm not good at eating much; I have an eating disorder.
- ✧ My family is poor; I go to bed and come to school hungry.
- ✧ My past situation has left me traumatized (or my current situation is terrible).
- ✧ People bully me.
- ✧ Someone in my family is abusing me sexually.
- ✧ There are too many noises at school; it hurts my ears, a lot.

If your worry isn't listed here, please write or draw it in the space below:

. . . .

. . . .

. . . .

. . . .

If you relate to these any of these statements, put the words into your worry basket or computer folder and start the process of chopping these big issues into smaller chunks.

A great way to unravel your big problem is to make it smaller. Have you heard the phrase, 'You can't eat the elephant whole?' This means that smaller problems are easier to digest than bigger ones. Apologies to vegetarians and vegans – I am not seriously suggesting that we eat elephants! Get comfy, grab something to write with, take a deep breath and be prepared to chop your big worry into small bits and to throw each of those bits into your virtual or actual worry basket.

If we're about breaking down the big thing, you need to give some examples of the sorts of things that are creating your stress. *Break the big thing into smaller things.*

For example, break your stress into two words that explain your stress:

My boyfriend + My body

Then try two more words.

Here are some examples of how your inner worry may sound in your head:

I love my boyfriend. He listens to my problems, but my family don't like him. I don't know what to do.

I hate my body. I need to make myself thinner, so my boyfriend doesn't leave me.

My family don't like my boyfriend.

I need to talk to mum when dad's at work, as he gets angry so quickly.

I need to make myself thin, so my boyfriend doesn't leave me.

I don't want to eat at school as I'm scared of eating the chips and getting fat. The food in the canteen is so fattening...

I'm so hungry when I get home I start to binge eat. I feel so ashamed. I don't want to face anyone, not even my friends.

I'm so worried about getting big. I can't go to school where everyone is eating.

I'm so worried about my exams. I can't sleep, and getting up in the morning for school makes me feel so tired.

See? We've taken the big word STRESS and broken it into lots of other words. We are starting to unfold or 'check out' our worry basket like we would take small items out of a shopping basket and put them in another bag to take home. We're starting to make our big issue into something that we can manage. A BIG problem has become a number of smaller issues.

When you're ready, have a look at the list below of possible reasons you just can't go to school even if you want to. Have a good look and see if you can relate to any of these, and share them with your trusted adult as soon as you can. Go through them one by one, using this workbook to help you. Use your conversation starters to encourage your trusted adult to listen.

How you feel about yourself:

 ♦ You're worried about your appearance.
 ♦ You haven't got lots of friends.
 ♦ You feel sad or cry a lot.

School:

 ♦ Is your teacher strict?
 ♦ Is there a particular bully at school? Or do you feel bullied by someone or a group of people at school?
 ♦ Do you find the lessons difficult to understand?
 ♦ Do you feel super-nervous in class?
 ♦ Do you feel ashamed if you get something wrong or don't know the answer?
 ♦ Are you in a new school, or have you moved from primary to high school/secondary school?
 ♦ Do you find learning difficult?

The circle of control

Write or draw any other school-related worries or issues in the circle that follows:

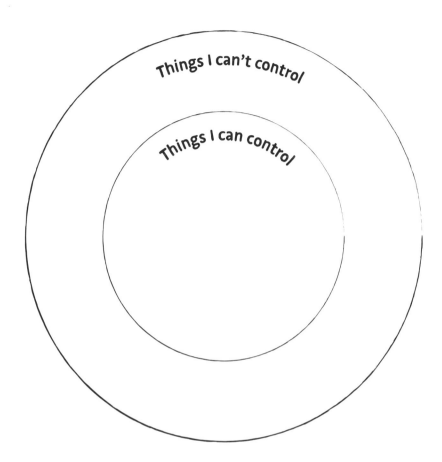

Issues at home:

- ✧ Family member, brother or sister is ill.
- ✧ Issues with your parents.
- ✧ Are you acting as a carer for someone else in your family, either a younger person or an older one, even your parent or carer?
- ✧ Is someone hurting you or touching you in a way that makes you uncomfortable?

Write or draw any other home-related worries or issues in the space below:

. . . .

. . . .

. . . .

. . . .

Your environment or issues outside of home:

Sometimes things happen around you, in your environment, that create storms of uncertainty in your life, such as a family member falling ill, or moving to another part of the country or even to a new country.

Life can create uncertainty that can feel like being swept up in a storm

◇ Do you have a new teacher or a new member of staff at school?
◇ Is there someone new in your class?
◇ Do you live in a city or town that feels unsafe or scary?
◇ Has someone in your family got into trouble with the law? Are they in prison?
◇ Has a family member lost their job?
◇ Do you need to move where you live in a hurry for any reason?
◇ Do your friends want you to skip school? Do they do bad

things – taking or selling drugs? Are they into other crimes such as burglary, shoplifting or county lines, or any other activities that may be against the law?

✧ Is someone in your close family group involved in criminal activity?

✧ Is someone in your close family group hurting someone else, or even hurting you?

✧ Do you live further away from school and does your family find it hard to get you or your brothers or sisters to school on time, every day?

✧ Are you nervous about travelling to school and back alone?

✧ Do you have enough money on your travelcard?

Write or draw any other outside of home-related worries or issues in the space below:

. . . .

. . . .

. . . .

Write or draw anything happening in the world around you that worries you that I haven't included in my previous lists:

. . . .

. . . .

. . . .

If your trusted adult has listened carefully to you, and they have a clear idea of what your problems are, together you can start to build a detailed plan to sort all of these things out. Although this won't be a magic wand, and you may have to do things that feel uncomfortable, you will be supported, and the feeling of achievement will be 100% worth it!

You get the picture...you start with a big issue like STRESS...and break it into smaller bits until you have lots of tiny issues to put in your worry basket. Small worries are much easier to deal with than big ones. And there is usually always someone you can speak to you about your small problems. There is also this magic thing that happens when you break a BIG problem into lots of small issues – the overwhelm lifts and you start to breathe again.

The basket is expandable, which means it can fit EVERYTHING in it, so don't worry about having too many worries – it will hold all of them. This is a process you will need to REPEAT, though, as there are always problems in life, and school life is especially complicated.

If your trusted adult has missed something or there is more, try a quick refresh with your ABCs (**A**ffirmation, **B**reathwork and **C**onversations, on page 23), as this might help you get going. It's important for the adult to create a plan with you to tackle your real issues rather than the issues they think you have! And it's important that you start off together and are clear about what you need to tackle together or with other adult helpers.

Don't forget, you'll need to have a worry bin too. Ask a teacher or parent if you can use an old shopping basket or wastepaper bin – it's great fun!

This is probably the most important part of the workbook as these are the techniques that you can use to get release from your worries.

When you have worked out what your problem is...

1. Break it into smaller issues you can work with (bite-sized chunks).

2. Discuss it.
3. Decide whether the worry is something inside of or outside of your control.
4. Act on it (when you're ready).
5. Now it's time to put it behind you.
6. Throw it away!

5

How and Why Anxiety Shows Up in Your Body

Trigger – thought – action – behaviour – consequence

When you understand the science of anxiety, it's much easier to 'step outside' of your anxiety, and you can then start to understand what's going on with your *body* as well as your *mind*.

Trigger – thought – action – behaviour – consequence (TTABC) is basically the chain reaction that takes place in everyone; it's how we all behave. The thing is, it all happens so quickly we don't notice it, because it's happening inside us in a complex network of nerves that stretches from the brain, through the spine, all the way down to the tips of our toes and fingers. It's called the central nervous system.

Salima shares the sorts of things that create anxiety in her, especially at school:

 I tend to be quite misunderstood; others think I'm overbearing/annoying. I don't see myself as being valued as a desirable friend/person to be friends or in a relationship with. I generally have low self-esteem and don't think highly of myself with anything.

Pixie's mum told me about how her daughter's school anxiety, which led to her school avoidance, started:

 It started really early, from day 2 of secondary school, she didn't want to go in. It became a daily battle and the advice from school was if a child doesn't want to come in due to anxiety, you have to get her in, because the longer she stays out, the harder it becomes. We had started to get her assessed for autism, the school was saying this, the educational psychologist was saying that. I could see she was traumatized. I thought no, I'm **not** pushing her to do something she's uncomfortable doing. We tried to protect her from the sensory overload of the classroom, and I don't regret her missing out on that kind of pain every day.

Marchelle explains how her shyness and autism create anxious feelings:

Sometimes when I'm around other people and I say something, I feel like I'm a tiny bit dumb, like I don't know anything. And when I say things, people look at me like they're thinking, what is she talking about? I feel a bit stupid, I always feel awkward, actually.

Do you remember the nursery rhyme, 'Little Miss Muffet'? This is a great illustration of how our nervous system works (the interlinked network of veins, nerves and blood vessels that runs right the way through the body, from our head through to the tips of our fingers and toes, carrying electrical messages, which affect how we feel and what we do – awesome, huh?):

Nursery rhyme	(what is happening)
Little Miss Muffet	(chilled little girl)
Sat on her tuffet	(comfortable)
Eating her curds and whey	(relaxed and calm)
Along came a spider	(trigger)
Who sat down beside her	(thought – this spider may be dangerous, I'm scared)
And frightened Miss Muffet away.	(action – runs away)

The following lines below are not in the original nursery rhyme.
Screaming help, OMG!!	(behaviour)
Curds and whey is uneaten,	
Miss Muffet is hungry and still	(consequence)
scared of spiders	

Things you can do for yourself

Imagine you're outside on a hot day and you've got a ridiculously heavy coat on and you feel so uncomfortable and so hot, like you could really do with taking that coat off? Then, when you take the coat off, you go PHEEEWWWW – that's better! That's what it's like when you talk to someone and start to unbottle those heavy feelings you've been carrying around with you – it's like taking off that heavy coat!

Once you start talking, you realize that your anxiety is starting to fade away. Talking to adults about your worries and fears can really help, but only if they truly listen. The good news is, that there are a few things you can do for yourself that will help you to untangle some of the complicated thoughts and feelings you may have. **Try out this fun activity.**

1. Create a box or tin of worries and a box or tin of dreams. You can make these boxes out of an empty tissue box or an old tin. Tins are a great idea as some can hold a lot of stuff and be fun to look at. I've spotted old Dalek tins and Quality Street tins in charity shops that are great for storing your favourite things, or ask an auntie or uncle or family elder – they always have tins!

2. Write down your fears and worries. Fold them up small and put them in the box or tin.

3. Write down on another piece of paper how your fear or worry gets sorted, and what you need to get your fear or worry sorted, and put that in your box or tin too.

4. For your box or tin of dreams, write down what needs to happen to make your dream come true and what you need to make it happen. Perhaps you need more pocket money, or singing lessons, or new pens, or a new bike or computer? Print off pictures and put them in your dream box or tin, along with your ideas and plans for getting what you dream about.

    Write as much detail as you can about your dream, how old you will be when your dream comes true, what will happen, who else will be involved in it, what you will be wearing, how it will help other people, where you will be living, how you will feel, and so on.

When strong emotions take over

Warning: This section might upset you. Maybe you could read it with your trusted adult, or with an adult close by.

'Self-harm' is a catch-all description for anything you do that makes you feel better for a short time, but over time can be extremely dangerous to you, and may even put your life in danger.

When the stress gets too much and you think that no one in the world understands you or that nothing will change, you may feel the urge to self-harm. Lots of young people start to self-harm to take away some of the pain of feeling stuck, not listened to and misunderstood.

The frustration of not being understood is real. Holding on to all those feelings of sadness, anger, guilt, confusion, depression and feeling 'different' is real. But the worst feeling of all is not knowing how to deal with those feelings or where to put them. Lots of young people self-harm in whatever way brings relief from those uncomfortable feelings.

If you're feeling really sad, you may not notice that you are feeling so helpless and alone that you can't see any point in living anymore and just want the pain to stop. Or you may be feeling so sad that you want to hurt yourself.

You may be aware of these types of self-harm: cutting, over-eating, over-the-counter medication, taking stuff you can buy from the local pharmacy (such as painkillers), taking illegal medication (weed, smoke, tabs), skin picking, hair or eyelash pulling, alcohol, anorexia, restrictive eating, bulimia (over-eating and making yourself sick afterwards) – and that's not everything.

You can self-harm in private, and successfully hide it from the adults around you. And, like school avoidance, self-harm may provide some temporary relief to your problem, but as it goes on, it will become a bigger problem in itself.

Say, for example, you are feeling stressed about your parents' divorce and you want to stay at home so your dad won't leave, which means going to school is out of the question. Both your parents want you to go to school, but you're too scared to tell them the *real* reason why you want to stay at home. Mum is getting angry with you because she's getting letters from school about your attendance. You're in a jam. You start with a small glass of vodka from the drinks cupboard. It's such a small amount, no one will notice. It's such a rush, and in a few minutes, all of your problems disappear. You tell your mum you don't feel well (which is partly true), so she lets you stay at home. It's then a shock to see the vodka bottle is three-quarters empty! You use all of your pocket money to buy another bottle. Now you feel guilt and shame about the drinking, not going to school and lying to your parents...

You can see it's easy to get into a negative self-harm cycle, when the thing you do to take away the pain becomes a thing itself.

Repeated self-harm can be treated with help from a qualified psychologist or psychiatrist. If you're under 16 (in the UK) you will need adult help to get an appointment; if you're over 16 you can self-refer for an appointment (see the 'Online Help and Resources' at the end of the book). It's important to get help as soon as you notice that your self-harm habit is getting out of control. Get early help so the habit doesn't cause you too much long-term harm.

You may feel so low and sad about your situation that you may be considering taking your own life. If you haven't shared how low you are feeling, you urgently need a plan to *make yourself safe*. See the 'Online Help and Resources' for emergency contacts.

One way to get out of this self-harm cycle is to find the words to explain and share your distress with the key people around you. Check Chapter 2 again to refresh yourself on these techniques.

Mood thermometer

You can keep a record of your strong or 'hot' feelings by making a mood thermometer:

> When hot and angry is 5
> Hot and tearful is 4
> Feeling neutral and okay is 3
> Feeling a bit down is 2
> Feeling totally depressed is a 1.

Have a go at drawing your mood thermometer, using the information above. You could colour in each number from 1 to 5. What colour would your hot and angry be? What colour would your totally depressed be? There is no right or wrong; this is your personal scale, so be as creative as you want.

My mood thermometer:

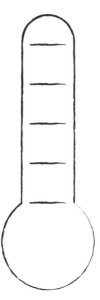

Try to see you if you can figure out what sorts of events send you to a 5, what makes you feel totally down at a 1 or 2, and how often you feel each mood. You can track this on your phone by putting a number next to every day of the week. It will also help you when you're talking to counsellors or therapists, so they can understand more about how you're feeling, and they can help you.

Phew, well done – you've worked so hard in this chapter and covered a lot of serious stuff. You may want to read bits of this chapter again, especially if worries are still sliding around in your head.

Ever Been to a Place Called 'Dread'?

There are many entry points in your life for the 'Dread' monster to appear. Actually, dread usually starts as a nagging worry that makes you feel stressed out, which can lead to anxiety if it goes on for a long time. Before you know it, you exist in a state of dread. NOT good. This chapter is going to show you how to reduce dread down to size, into smaller 'dread-lets' that are less scary and easier to manage.

Let's start with the dictionary meaning of 'dread': '*anticipate* with great *apprehension* or *fear*'. This means:

> *Anticipate*: wait for something to happen.
> *Apprehension*: anxiety or fear that something bad will happen.
> *Fear* (abstract noun): not a real thing, but a *feeling*.

These are pretty powerful words that can describe how RUBBISH you feel, but they're not concrete things. In other words, *dread, fear, apprehension, anxiety* and *worry* are simply words (abstract nouns, actually) that name something you cannot see, hear, touch, smell or taste.

The real power here is the emotions behind these words. Even though emotions feel real, because human beings are amazing, we can learn how to *manage* or *tame* our stronger emotions. As far as I know, humans are the only species of animals that can do this. This is useful, so our emotions don't end up controlling us. Read this a few times, because when you get your head around this, it's MEGA.

We can:

✧ Block (inhibit) things out that upset us
✧ Self-soothe – rock, dance, cry, touch
✧ Re-focus our attention (distract or reappraise the event)
✧ Modify and substitute for a more healthy emotion (e.g., 'Instead of hitting the wall, I can paint, sing, draw or play the guitar, which will shift me to a happier feeling').

Before we learn to manage our emotions, we need to understand where they are coming from or what is causing them. As human beings, we are affected by what is going on in our lives that is 'external' to us – in other words, in the *environment* around us.

Some examples of external causes of our sadness might be:

✧ Where we live – is it a small house? Are there enough beds for everyone?
✧ Food – do you have enough food? Do you ever go to bed hungry at night?
✧ Safety – do you feel safe from harm, either at home or at school or anywhere else?
✧ Do you think your life is in danger in any way?
✧ Do you feel safe from harm at home?
✧ Does your house have leaks or are there other things about your home that make you worry?
✧ Do you feel safe walking to and from school or the bus stop or anywhere else on your school journey?
✧ Do you see gang members near where you live?
✧ Have you moved home recently and still feel unsure about your surroundings?

All of these issues are neatly summed up in this cool diagram created by a Russian psychologist called Abraham Maslow. The triangle shape that explains it is called 'Maslow's hierarchy of needs'.

You can see that we need the bottom of the triangle to be quite wide to meet all of our basic needs, including food, shelter and safety. If we are lucky to have a home, we still need to feel safe in our home, and to feel loved, and wanted. And so on, until we get to the top of the triangle, which is where we feel we are truly ourselves; we feel respected, heard and are doing what makes us feel happy and truly fulfilled as human beings. The feeling of being at the top of the triangle, at the peak of human experience and self-expression, is what most of us strive to achieve in our lives. At the very top of the triangle we feel so confident and happy with ourselves that we almost don't need approval from others! It's very likely that people will 'look up' to us.

So, we've established that dread is fear of what hasn't happened yet; it's an extreme form of worry. Dread is 'next-level' worry. Although you can use the breathing techniques from Chapter 2, you first need to unlock your feelings of dread, which basically means untangling all of your worries that are knotted into a big grey ball. Once you start to untangle your messy feelings, you will find it easier to cope with your everyday ups and downs.

You may have been in a car accident, lived in a war zone, been diagnosed with a rare illness or experienced the death of a close relative. Whatever you've lived through has left a scar on your heart that is making it hard to adjust to daily life. This level of dread is totally understandable and is known as PTSD (post-traumatic stress disorder). You are likely to experience intense feelings in your body, such as rage and extreme anger. Or, at the other end of the emotional scale, you may feel total numbness, like you are just going through the motions of life. There but not really there. People may comment that you seem cold. This emotional distance or 'shutdown' is a sign that the shock hasn't left your body (see Chapter 3). You might totally 'zone out' of some experiences and be unable to cope with others and have no idea why. You need professional help to move your body and mind out of this 'frozen' emotional state. Try not to worry, though, as PTSD is treatable.

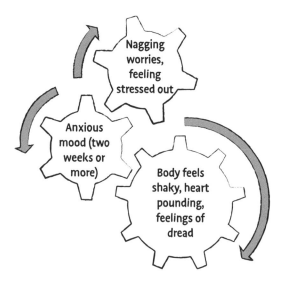

Talk through each of the four stages leading up to dread with your adult:

1. Nagging worries, feeling stressed out.
2. Anxiety (carries on for more than two or three weeks).
3. Physical symptoms of paralysing dread (sweaty palms, sick in the pit of your stomach).
4. The dread is so bad that you stop (or avoid) certain activities for fear it will get worse.

If you have reached the stage of paralysing dread (number 3), you've probably had worries that have made you feel stressed out and anxious for a number of months, years even. If you've had intense anxious feelings, the sort that create changes in your daily life that affect your eating habits, sleeping patters, mood or ability to concentrate, it's likely that you've held on to these feelings and have not been able to talk them through for a number of reasons. It may be several weeks or even months before you can be upbeat again, because you've been carrying the weight of your sad feelings around for so long.

When you were at school, you may have learned about the five senses – taste, touch, sound, sight and smell. If you're highly sensitive, you may be aware of a few other senses, such as the feeling inside your body when you're nervous or the feeling of being off-balance or of movement in your body and joints that helps you to sense space around you or how you can touch your elbow with your eyes shut!

An occupational therapist (OT) can show you exercises that will help you to calm your nervous system when your body feels at odds with itself. These can involve equipment or soft toys, blankets, pillows, blocks and a range of other specialist items that will:

✧ Stimulate or strengthen parts of your body
✧ Apply pressure or sensations that soothe
✧ Make you feel balanced and quietened down, or may even 'turn off' some of your big emotions.

An OT can also help if you are having issues at school with noise, getting comfortable at your desk, finding your way around the school building, eating, going to the toilet, and lots more. If you have issues with any of these areas that cause you to feel worried, an OT is a great expert for you and your family to talk to, depending on what your body needs.

Here are a few examples of other therapeutic activities or items to investigate that help bring body and mind into more harmony:

✧ Baking
✧ Balancing
✧ Beads

✧ Bean bags
✧ Crunchy snacks
✧ Essential oils
✧ Felt
✧ Fiddle toys.

And here are a few activities that will excite or calm your senses if your mood is low:

I hope this chapter has got you curious about how doing activities that involve the senses and the body can help you to feel calmer, energized, or just a bit less sad.

7

When Adults Make Demands

EXPLORING BEHAVIOUR, AUTISM, PATHOLOGICAL DEMAND
AVOIDANCE AND OBSESSIVE-COMPULSIVE DISORDER

Pixie highlights the difficulties she faced when moving from primary
to secondary school:

> My school avoidance started after primary school, when I was 12, and I don't
> remember a lot of it, because it was quite hard, so I've just forgotten it. I came
> home on my last day of primary school and was so upset. I didn't have a good
> time in that year (Year 6 primary). I had a new teacher; everyone was acting a bit
> different, a bit full of themselves. It got worse, my teacher was loud, the boys were
> causing a riot, and her way of dealing with it was to yell at them. I have sensory
> processing disorder and very good hearing. The teacher was screaming at them,
> I couldn't really be in the classroom. I started leaving school around an hour or
> half an hour early; my nana would come and pick me up.

When you feel stressed or upset, your mood affects your behaviour. You
either 'act out' by distracting your mates, being noisy, silly or disruptive,
or you turn in and become quiet, withdrawn and distant from the rest
of the class. Neither of these reactions is better or worse; they both
make you feel rotten. But kids who tend to act out are often excluded
because their behaviour is noticed and causes problems for the teacher
and the other pupils.

Marchelle was described as a child with behaviour difficulties, and
even though she was diagnosed with autism, she was excluded from
school several times:

Mostly the teachers put me with the SLT [senior leadership team] – the SLT would be like a detention. I would stay there all day every day. I didn't really like going there; sometimes it would be for doing nothing and it made me feel, I don't know, really sad. There were lots of teachers who would be rude to me or shout at me.

Marchelle was upset when she was telling me about her experience:

Schools don't really understand how I feel. I moved around to a lot of schools, when I was in Year 7, I stopped going to school. And when I was in Year 8, I got put into a PRU [Pupil Referral Unit]. There were a lot of boys there and I felt uncomfortable, so I left there, then I started doing tutoring at home. After the home tutoring, I went to a college for children with social, emotional and behavioural issues, as well as for children with ASD [autism spectrum disorder] or ADHD [attention-deficit hyperactivity disorder].

There is a specific condition called pathological demand avoidance (PDA), which sounds intense. Evidence shows that PDA is linked to autism spectrum condition, and looks to other people like you are being really stubborn by showing extreme *avoidance* of everyday tasks. Requests like getting ready for bed, going to the shops or going to school are met with extreme resistance, anger, outbursts and sometimes a flat 'No, I'm not doing it, don't ask me again'.

Young people with PDA can be smart, funny and with fantastic communication skills, but don't be fooled. Behind their fun personality, they can feel chronically anxious and use their extreme behaviour to hide or 'mask' their unhappiness and pretend everything is okay. Lots of children and young people who are autistic or who have PDA are either excluded from or don't go to school. Whatever your diagnosis, school can seem like a long list of demands, and they all stress you out.

Pixie picks up the theme:

It would have been easier to go to school, but my feeling is the root of the problem is the education system! The environment was so stressful, from the boys to the noise and some of the teachers not understanding me. I'm sure the reason lots of children don't go to school is because in some cases it is damaging them! I knew a few boys who were autistic, and they were in years ahead of me, and they were different to me. But it should be so easy to let people be the way they are, it's frustrating. My teachers acted like I should be ashamed of being autistic and they were comforting me. Their pitying could have triggered feelings of insecurity in me, but I was never really insecure about it, but they're our teachers! If they knew how my class teacher was shouting – they didn't get that she didn't know, it didn't click with her that that was an issue; if they were a bit more understanding…

School exclusion

Statistically, more boys are excluded from school than girls, and more girls avoid school. The data is complex to unpick and it isn't always about good or bad behaviour; it's more about how welcome or understood children feel when they're at school. If you've been excluded from school, you may feel unable to go back. Being excluded is a traumatic experience, and whatever the cause of your exclusion, you should attend your re-introduction meeting to see how you can move forward again. The school will outline their expectations about your return to school.

In this meeting they will also need to find out:

◇ Whether you fully understand the reason/s why you were excluded.
◇ How they will support your return to school (extra teachers, help in lessons, emotional support and so on…).

The school may need to identify if you have additional educational needs that require specialist support during the school day. They may also suggest that your requirements to learn at school are laid out in a document or plan that states exactly what you need to help you learn, and how exactly you will get that help in school and who will deliver this help. The school may need to apply to your local council or voluntary agencies for this additional support.

If this is what needs to happen after your exclusion, it is actually a good thing, although it may not feel like it at the time. It is positive because the teachers will understand more about why you were excluded and won't think that you were just being 'naughty'. The flip side is that you may feel embarrassed about receiving extra support in school, especially if you're worried about your mates teasing you, but if they tease you about getting extra help to learn, guess what? They might be nicer to you if they understand what your struggles are, and if they still tease you, it might be time to think about the sort of people you pick to be your friends. Getting the right support, even after an exclusion, can really turn it around for you and make school a much better place.

Being excluded involves more than just the 'naughty' child; the events that lead up to an exclusion include the teacher and the other pupils in the class. Pixie's mum spoke warmly of a teacher who seemed to have a great instinct for *all* of his pupils:

> We had one great teacher, he encouraged Pixie in creative writing, and those who were good at sport, he just got it. I've never met a single person who didn't thrive in his class. A lot of it is personality as well. A lot of teachers forget that children are whole people already; they have the same feelings – sometimes a lot more intense.

If you're reading this and you have a *neurodivergent* brain (whoa...long word alert!!!! Neurodivergent means having a brain that works differently to other people's. Neuro – relating to the brain – divergent – relating to difference from the majority, such as being autistic or having dyslexia), you will certainly experience the world in your own different, magical way. You are likely to have knock-out *strengths or talents* in some areas – maybe dance, science, art or maths – and some difficulties or challenges in other areas – such as concentration and making friends.

Pixie continued:

> One of my teachers said you're only 'mildly' autistic. I got my diagnosis in the evening and I went into school the next day to tell the teacher. The Resource teacher was a lovely woman, but she did the whole 'but you're only very mildly autistic!' No one would guess you're autistic, and everyone was tiptoeing around me – I don't CARE if everyone knows I'm autistic – but it was the whole 'you don't act autistic', and everyone was making it sound like I should be way more upset about it than I actually was. Don't comfort me about something I'm not upset about – it's FINE [laughs, but clearly irritated]. It was weird, I couldn't

understand why people were comforting me, 12 hours after my diagnosis; I was 12 years old and didn't really understand what it meant to me.

I asked Pixie's mum how her daughter's experience felt for her:

What I would say to other parents is trust your child. The school may try to talk you into doing things, but if it feels wrong, chances are, it is wrong. It's hard to see your child struggling but there is light at the end of the tunnel – there were some mornings when I thought this light was getting further away, but if you've got a child who loves learning, it's hard to see them not get the education they're entitled to or they deserve. Keep fighting, which is exhausting; keep trusting your child. Some people would say it's the mum; if it was that easy, she would be in school and so would my son. And reaching out to other parents who are the same boat is very helpful too. It always seems to be the mums [who attend the school meetings and try to organize the support and so on].

If you have a different sort of brain, one that thinks in colours or likes to organize things or thinks very fast and makes you want to move around a lot or struggles ordering letters and reading (dyslexic) or finds numbers hard to recognize and compute with (dyscalculia) or finds coordinating their everyday movements difficult (dyspraxia), it's likely that you've experienced:

◇ Bullying
◇ Learning difficulties
◇ Friendship problems.

Pixie picks up the theme:

If teachers had more of an up-to-date training about autism, that would help, and I'd like to know who was giving that training; it certainly wasn't an autistic person!

Marchelle talks about being misunderstood and finding it as difficult to understand her friends as they find it difficult to understand her. Being neurodivergent is like this – having such different experiences of the world that it feels like you are speaking different languages. Imagine if some people experience things in colour, and other people experience things in sounds. Both sorts of people might be able to get along, but they won't 'mesh' in the same way that two people with colourful brains will and two musical brains would.

They're both brains, but they use different *operating systems*, so the degree of 'overlap' between them is going to be less than two brains using a similar operating system. No brain type is 'better' than another; they are just not entirely compatible, in the same way the different brain types will have different areas of strengths and weaknesses. I hope this helps you to understand the basics of neurodiversity.

As Pixie said:

I found it hard going into school; going into a class of five-year olds was easier than being with my peers. One particular teacher was amazing, she did things that I don't even think the school knew about.

All of these issues can make you feel tense, which can result in emotional outbursts of anger at school. Sometimes your anger is due to the mean things that people have said to you, and other times it's just because being YOU feels so hard. If your teacher or doesn't know about your challenges, they will just see the explosion and think 'Oh there goes X, kicking off again! Every time they kick off, it disrupts the whole class and I get behind on my lesson plan for that year group.' Or your classmates might think: 'Why doesn't she just do what she's told instead of getting so upset?'

Does that sound like you? I thought so. This is why using your voice calmly to explain how life is for you is really important. Some of the problems you are having might not even be your fault. And if you tell the right people, you will get help for those problems, which will give you time to work out what you're good at.

If you find it difficult to express yourself using words, working with a speech and language therapist (SaLT) can help. They are trained to help you express yourself by finding and using the best communication skills that are important for school life. They are great to have on your team!

Studies show that many neurodivergent youngsters – those with conditions that influence the way they think, feel and experience the world – also struggle to stay mentally healthy. This can mean just being you is more tiring for you than for your friends. I want to say to you straight up that feeling anxiety, depression, having obsessive-compulsive disorder (OCD), panic attacks and other mental health difficulties are NOT part of being neurodivergent or differently wired. They are, however, more common for the following reasons:

◇ Society is taking a long time to catch up with how to properly include ALL people in our environment, and in many places – including schools – things can go wrong due to carelessness, lack of understanding or not even knowing how to act fairly to all people in all settings.

◇ Teachers in school have differing levels of knowledge about neurodivergent learners, and what sorts of things they can do to make school more comfortable for them. It's worrying to hear from the students I chat to that some teachers don't really listen to them when they try to explain their issues.

Or if they do listen, they don't really understand, or they fail to put in place the sorts of things that would actually help. We need more training and softer approaches to solve this problem. I don't believe anyone learns anything when they're unhappy.

◇ Often when you feel that you are at fault, the problem could be with a particular teacher, or your peer group bullying or teasing you. Sometimes the barriers to going to school are actually in the school building, environment or certain people. This workbook will help you to be clear about what is making you unhappy and wanting to avoid school, and I truly hope that the adults around you will support you in trying to fix whatever problem or problems you are experiencing with school. You can do things to manage your moods or anxiety, but the school teachers and other school kids need to do their bit too. ☺

◇ Because neurodivergent young people have to work so hard to fit in and be understood, it can be exhausting, and cause higher levels of stress than other people have to face.

◇ Some scientists and researchers believe that different brain types are especially vulnerable to mental health challenges, with some stating that these sorts of problems can run in families – in some families there are patterns of particular difficulties that run in the family, from grandparent to parent to child.

Marchelle was willing to tell me her story – we chatted for nearly two hours!

I went to a special needs school with mixed ability children. It was boring for me, and I really wanted to learn but it was really hard, as none of the teachers really understood. I'm now in another college; some of the teachers are so uneducated about autism. One of my teachers said, 'Is it true that people with autism know what they're doing but do it anyway? Autism is a mental health disorder, I learned that when I was training.' I told her she was getting her information from a book.

Marchelle went on:

...not from real life. She acts as if she knows everything. She's taking her information from a book, rather than listening to someone who is actually autistic who is in front of her. That's so annoying. I started my new college at the start of Year 10.

When I've done my GCSEs, I don't really know what I'd like to do; my family always tell me what to do, I don't really want to be a doctor or a lawyer. Even though I know how to argue well, I want to do a profession that I like personally. Not something that my family want me to do, just because they want me to make a lot of money. At soon as I went into Year 10, I went to my current school. I will not be going to the sixth form.

I asked Marchelle if there were any particular people who made attending school difficult for her:

I used to get picked on, because I'm a giving person. I would give people a lot of money; they would say to me 'Oh I'm really hungry Marchelle'. I would say to them I have money, I can pay for you, so I'd do that. There were people who picked on me and called me 'skinny' and then I stopped eating a little bit and I got really skinny... I don't really have any people to talk to, I don't usually talk to people, I'm usually at home. I bottle my feelings up 'cos no one really understands, so I don't really speak that much. I didn't like doing any work; when I work, and I think too much (I think people think I'm lying!!) my vision starts to fuzz up and my brain starts to hurt – not my actual brain but my head hurts. Especially when teachers say you can do it, you can do it! I don't know why they say that because they don't know how it feels.

I've actually never met autistic people that are like me, if that makes sense. It would be amazing to meet autistic people who have a personality that matches mine, that would be amazing!

What makes having a friendship harder is that I put a lot of expectations on people. If people don't fulfil my expectations, I will get really mad and I will get jealous really easily. I found out that two of my friends were invited to another friend's house and her boyfriend was there, but they didn't even invite me. I just found it so rude; the way I see things is that people should ask me, so I can say 'yes' or 'no', rather than just not be invited. I was upset because they were my closest friends and I felt really backstabbed. I feel like I'm not in the circle and I already feel not included, which makes me feel even more out of the circle. When I say stuff, I just say things without thinking.

I didn't feel guilty about not going to school; I felt happy, because going to school makes me feel really uncomfortable. I do like being around people and don't particularly like staying at home, but being at school still makes me uncomfortable. I don't like being around people – I like my own space, I like my own company. I can't really cope around people; it's just too much. But people say but you look fine, but that's only because I'm not showing.

In my first secondary school there was a history teacher, and I really liked him and there was a SEN [special educational needs] teacher. He was always nice to me, even though some teachers would shout at me; he was nice, he didn't shout at me.

My advice to any young autistic girl reading this would be to keep striving and don't let anybody's words upset you and to remember that you are always powerful regardless of what anyone says to you and you can do anything that you put your mind to.

Here are some extracts from Marchelle's letter to her current school:

1. Thank you for having me, but before you say you can cater for children with autism you should get your staff to be trained and really understand us more, as we're not hard to understand.
2. Listen to us speak as some of us find it really hard to tell you how we're feeling and what we're going through; they should understand that not all autistics have the same autism traits, looking out for kids that are extra smart, every autistic person is different in their own way. If teachers did care about their job, as much as they say they do, they would want to learn about each individual autistic child.
3. I was underestimated by the teachers because you don't always say what you think or feel. No one knows my true ways and I feel the school needs to cater for what they say they're going to do. They should let people be themselves rather than have to mask all the time.
4. Sometimes my brain is really blank, and I don't know how to start conversations, so I don't mind you leading the conversation and then I can just speak.

Can you relate to Marchelle's words?

. . . .

. . . .

. . . .

What sort of difficulties do you have making friends?

. . . .

. . . .

. . . .

If you're autistic, ADHD or dyslexic, or have another issue that means making friends difficult, what would help you?

. . . .

. . . .

. . . .

. . . .

. . . .

That was quite an intense read. I hope you find it comforting to see that other young people are having a difficult time at school and fitting in too.

A Bit More about Stress and How to Manage It

What is stress?

You might think that stress is in your head, right? When you have a 'lot on your mind'. Which is true. But stress also makes your *body* feel different, and your thoughts can lead to a physical reaction, based on an abstract thought. (Remember Little Miss Muffet?)

We react in one of five ways:

- ✧ *Fight*: we literally punch, hit out, slap, kick or use whatever part of our body we can to attack whatever is threatening us.
- ✧ *Flight*: this isn't actually flying, although if we were birds sensing danger, we would actually fly away. As humans don't have wings, not any that I know of anyway, instead of flying away for danger – we run! As fast as we can, and we keep going until we think we are far enough away from danger to be safe.
- ✧ *Freeze*: this is a strange reaction to something dangerous, but instead of running, some people are so frightened that they just can't move. Have you ever felt like that? It's scary, isn't it? A good example of this is when a spider rolls itself up into a little ball and pretends to be dead. (Most of the time they're not dead; they're just trying very hard to stay alive.)
- ✧ *Fawn*: this is an interesting response to stress. It's is all about making yourself soft and friendly and trying to please other people, even if you feel really angry inside.

✧ *Flop:* this is when your body goes into a sort of faint, or 'black out', which sounds really scary but it's your body's way of protecting you. It's the same as when some animals pretend to be dead to avoid being eaten or killed by their predators.

Which one of these stress reactions have you done? Can you remember the situation? Do you feel it worked for you?

. . . .

. . . .

. . . .

Our human stress response, the root cause of anxiety, has been with us for thousands of years, since pre-historic times, and was designed to keep us safe from danger. Here are some examples:

✧ We see a dangerous tiger nearby > we understand we could be the tiger's dinner (and tigers run fast) > blood rushes to our legs so our muscles are strong enough for us to take *flight* > we run away.
✧ We spot a dangerous bear in the distance > we understand that we could be the bear's dinner (the bear hasn't spotted us) > we *freeze* until the bear has gone in a different direction, our heart beats very fast in our chest and our breathing is shallow.
✧ An unknown creature is coming near to our nest where our babies are > we have no time to think but it looks like they're carrying a weapon > we raise up on our hind legs and *fight* for our lives – the blood rushes to our muscles to provide huge power if we need to hit out, and our thinking brain shuts down for a short while and the feelings or 'animal' brain takes over.

These responses happen so fast between the brain and the body that we don't even have to think about what to do. It's like switching on a light – it's pretty instant. Most of us won't face any of these threats that activate our primal nature – hardly any of us even live in the wilderness anymore! But our brains have been slow at keeping up with our hyper-fast human change. The 'alarm' gland in our brain is still fully charged and we spring into the same actions, even when someone...er... steals our pen at school. Or calls us a mean name. The danger to us is small yet we still have the BIG reactions programming.

The evolutionary process means that the ancient, deep part of our brain is still easily triggered, even when the 'danger' isn't actually a sabre tooth tiger – it's actually a test at school! If our ancient brain is activated too often, it can create 'bad stress' in our bodies, which isn't good for us if this happens too frequently.

GOOD STRESS

✦ Any sort of performance – school play, music exam, dance competition, rugby or football game, exam or test.

✦ A party or occasion with lots of people and noise and food – things that we worry about ('What if no one talks to me?' 'What if I don't like the food?'). Once you are there and have relaxed, found someone to talk to and something you like to eat, the stress goes away and you can start to enjoy yourself.

BAD STRESS

✦ A problem that won't go away, not knowing how to solve a problem, feeling scared of something or someone and keeping it to yourself.

✦ Experiencing a problem that you can't tell anyone about, so the problem stays there and makes you feel worse every day.

Doing an exam or speaking in a school assembly does not put us in the *danger zone*. The school assembly is an example where nervous tension is 'boosted' by adrenaline (a hormone released by your adrenal glands, which sit on top of your kidneys), which gives us a boost to help us focus and tackle the stress in a positive way and do our best.

A teeny, weeny history and science lesson

As a species, we have evolved so quickly that the 'alarm' system in our brains is overworking, making us stress out about things that are no longer life-threatening.

Why is being anxious for a long time bad for our health? The 'danger zone' of anxiety is due to the chemicals that are released into our bloodstream when we feel stressed: cortisol and adrenaline. When the adrenaline hormone *stays in our system for a long time*, it starts to wear us out. Imagine if you had to present an assembly every day for a whole year! You would find that exhausting and intense and the *constant stress* would create physical problems for you, including trouble sleeping, difficulty concentrating, irritability, tearfulness, bursts of anger, tummy upsets, feeling faint or a racing heart.

If you are experiencing this sort of emotional shutdown, you will find it very hard to respond positively to being asked to do something 'just because'. You feel better when you know what's coming and why; you like things to be predictable as this helps you to feel safe. I chatted to lots of young people just like you in order to understand more deeply why going to school can be so difficult. The reasons are as complicated and different as you all are, but the key messages I got from young people like you are:

◇ Listen to me.
◇ Believe me.
◇ Gain my trust and work with me.
◇ Give me time to take everything in.
◇ Don't push me too quickly.

I have talked about adults believing and really listening to you, and this is really the case for young people who find it impossible to do what they are asked to do. At school or at home, it's usual to be asked to do things by the adult who is responsible for you. If you don't do what you're asked, it's likely that you will get into trouble.

Imagine having a condition at school that means you are always getting into trouble because you don't do what the teachers say. You may have heard of PDA (pathological demand avoidance), which is a difficult and upsetting way of describing your actions that appear to be very defiant, but you can't help the way you feel. It's understandable that you wouldn't want to put yourself through that level of stress every day, so you stop going. Lots of young people with PDA are unable to go to school, as school involves a lot of teachers asking you to do something and you're expected to do it, no questions asked!

Do you think young people who are strong-minded, opinionated, curious and outspoken have a more difficult time from their teachers?

....

Do you think that schools and teachers are out of tune with young people?

....

....

What do you think would help?

....

....

....

Do you feel you can be yourself at school? If not, what or who do you think is stopping you?

....

....

....

....

If you think you have a neurodivergent brain, speak to an adult about this or do some online research with organizations that are expert in different brain types, such as the ADHD Foundation or the National Autistic Society or the regional or national autism or ADHD organization where you live. If you are 'masking' at school – trying to hide who you really are because you're afraid or ashamed to be different – it is important to talk to someone about this. Hiding who you are isn't good for you and can add to your anxiety.

Learning how your body and brain work together and how anxiety shows up in your body is complicated, but it's an important thing to learn. This is real chemistry, not in test tubes! Learning about human emotions and reactions will help you start to get some control of your own emotions, which is a great place to start.

Well done for getting this far!

When the Bullying and Peer Pressure Gets Too Much

Bullying is one of the many reasons why lots of children and young people find it difficult to get to school every day. If you have been bullied in the past, you may be storing those feelings of dread about it happening again in your body, which is another reason why you can 'shut down' and find it difficult to engage with school or trust people.

Considering that bullying is something that schools can tackle, it's sad that it persists in schools and can make a child's daily experience of life in school so miserable. The tricky thing about bullying is that it can be difficult to prove. And even if you can prove it, it's complicated. You don't want to look weak or make the bully mad because you were 'telling tales' or acting like a 'snitch', and if they think you're a 'snitch', this is another thing for them to bully you over on top of the original 'thing' they were bullying you for.

GOOD NEWS – there is a good way to break the cycle of bullying.

Beat bullies in five steps (notice, I didn't say 'easy' steps). It's not easy; in fact, the first step is usually the hardest, but when you've made that first step, the thrill you feel about starting to take your life back is amazing:

1. Find your brave self (or FAKE it) and say the following words out loud in a firm and clear voice: 'Go away and leave me alone!'
2. Look the bully in the eye, if you can, as you say it.
3. Walk away.

4. If they start up again you can say, 'You DON'T intimidate me' (or if you struggle to say that word, say, 'I am not scared of you, go away'!).

5. Reflect on your own bravery; remind yourself that no one should push you around and get away with it – repeat: 'I am good and deserve to be treated with respect'.

Try to stay calm, and use a slow and medium-to-loud voice, but not a shout, as this can trigger the bully to shout back and the situation could quickly get out of control. If there is more than one person bothering you, you MUST tell a trusted adult as well as a teacher.

If the bullying is taking place outside of school, that's more difficult, but if the people who are bullying you are in school uniform and are part of the school community, you may need to ask an adult to report serious physical bullying, or other criminal activity regarding drug misuse or trafficking, to other authorities. Every sort of bullying is serious and can affect your confidence as well as hurting you physically. It's an issue that the school needs to help you with.

Remember: you do not have to handle this situation on your own. If you stay away from school due to bullying, this means that the bully has proved their power over you. And not only that, but they are messing up your education. Think about it – you're giving away a lot of your power to someone who hasn't earned the right to control your life, right?

Changing your behaviour

There are two things you can do right now to start to feel better:

- ◇ Try to *change the negative* thoughts about yourself in your head.
- ◇ *Distract yourself from your sad thoughts* by actively turning your attention to things that make you feel better.

You may not feel better straight away, but if you try these techniques *regularly*, you will find you can cope better with your heavy feelings.

Whether you are a bully yourself or have been bullied at school and don't want to go to school, you may not realize that there are ways to change what happens to you. You have the option to REACT or RESPOND:

✧ A reaction is usually emotional – anger, outburst, physical – that comes from the ancient or 'animal' part of your brain.
✧ A response is usually rational – you've used your brain first before using your body; the response starts when you use your thinking brain.

Teachers and therapists are great at teaching you to switch from reacting to responding. Even if you've had a really horrible time up until now, there is still hope, there is still time to change some of the patterns, and there are lots of adults who can help you.

Here's a weird thing – brains can change, because they have plasticity (no, they're not made of Plasticine, but in their biology they are living organisms that can adapt to their environment). That's why we generally don't put our hands in hot flames as we have learned, and *remember*, that being burned *hurts*! It is possible to train or re-train your brain, so you have the opportunity to make some of your bad experiences less intense for you and some of your strong negative reactions can become weaker. With a great team around you, you can change from worrier to warrior!

If you practise the exercises in this workbook you can change from shy snail to social snail, if that's what you want. Become a friendly bee, buzzing around, doing what makes you happy, shining your natural colours (usually bright colours) and attracting new and nice people in the process. Avoiding things that hurt, like bullies or school, does make the pain go away, but only for a short while. At some point you will have to stop running away from your pain and run towards it and have a conversation with it!

Sometimes your parents will worry about how you will react to certain situations, especially if you've had difficult situations to deal with in the past, but if you keep avoiding them, it will become more difficult for you to grow a pair of strong horns, create your own protective fences or find your strong inner voice.

Something else you may be anxious about is getting into trouble with the teachers at school. It may sound odd, but when teachers get stressed and upset, they usually show it with anger. Do you have any ideas about how teachers could express their anger without shouting, especially if they are cross with you? Write them down or discuss them with your parent or support person:

. . . .

. . . .

. . . .

. . . .

Once you and your family have worked out what it is you are anxious about, this workbook will help you figure out a plan to get on top of your worry and eventually get it under control so you can live your life without these barriers. Life is like a computer game – there are always barriers to overcome and tall walls to climb over without falling, and that's what makes them fun and exciting.

Write some of your worry words on the balloons (e.g., stress, sadness, anger).

Have fun bursting these balloons barriers when you start to talk about and tackle your worries.

If you're a sensitive person, you can imagine that you're a sponge, sucking up other people's worries and meanness and anger. Every now and again you need to squeeze out that sponge.

When you're older, you can learn about ways to 'block' the negative energy of others, especially if they mean you harm. Do this balloon exercise every day, if possible, to encourage your brain to re-programme itself to help you heal and start experiencing each day with more ease. And making your problems disappear by popping them like a balloon is fun.

You could also try repeating affirmation exercises, which are so powerful – use them as soon as the jittery feelings start:

'This feeling is my anxiety washing through me; it will eventually pass.'

'It feels horrible, so I will make myself comfortable with a blanket/a hot drink/a book/some chill music, etc., and wait for it to pass.' (Choose whatever works for you.)

'If my mind starts wondering on the bad stuff, I will use some of my distraction activities, such as listening to the songs on my happy playlist.'

'Okay thoughts, you've said enough, now what?'

'If they still haven't gone away, I will go to my virtual worry basket, take out this named worry and see if I can split it into smaller pieces.'

This process is called 'sitting' with your anxiety, using an anxiety recovering routine – which may sound totally weird, but here is how it works:

◇ Accept the feeling (don't try to get rid of it – you feel anxious, have done for a while, that's the way it is right now).
◇ Worry doesn't change a THING! It just makes you feel worse. Imagine throwing logs on a fire that you're trying to put out.
◇ Sitting with the feeling seems weird, but it works by putting you in charge of the feelings rather than the feelings overwhelming you.
◇ Doing something kind for yourself while you sit with the

uncomfortable feelings encourages your stressed-out body to calm down too.

✧ Commit to make small changes to help yourself recover.

**Sitting with your feelings helps you calm down and
work out what you can and can't change
Sit with your emotions when they arise, feel them, listen to them, appreciate
them, never run from them or they will track you down until you are courageous
enough to face them and ultimately learn the lesson they hold**

Q. Why is it important to stick to an anxiety recovery routine like this?

A. Because feelings of low mood and depression can become strong and unbearable. When we feel like this, we often don't want to do anything to help ourselves feel better. Sticking to a self-care routine when you feel like you can't be bothered to do anything else is a great first step. And you know what comes after the first step, don't you...? YES! The second, third and fourth steps – YAY! You're on your way!

Giving you time to shine

It may seem difficult at first, but if you do this every time you have a panic attack or intense feelings of panic or dread, you will start to notice yourself come out of it more quickly.

Wow! You are working so hard – I see you, champion!

Your Ideal School

This chapter is about designing a place that would suit you for learning. Have you ever thought about building design? What sorts of things make a school building feel safe, interesting, calm or exciting? Thinking about your ideal school is a fun exercise as it allows you to explore ideas about what would make 'your ideal school'.

To help you get started, take five minutes to think about all of the things you *don't like* about your school building. For lots of young people, the whole idea of school is heavy, with unpleasant and scary symbols, like a horror story! For example, think about the lights, the toilets, the playground, the dining hall, the indoor PE area – what areas make you feel stressed or scared?

. . . .

. . . .

. . . .

Write or add to this list of places in your school building that make you feel yuk!

. . . .

. . . .

. . . .

Here are some questions to ask yourself as you start this exercise.

Environment:

◇ Does any part of the school experience make you feel warm and safe?
◇ Are there any parts of the school building you don't like?
◇ Which do you prefer – being at home or at school?
◇ Do you wish your school was smaller or bigger?
◇ Would you like to be somewhere else during the day instead of school?
◇ Do you think the noise levels at school are okay?
◇ Do you think there are good reasons for teachers needing to shout at school?
◇ Do you hate communal changing rooms at school?
◇ Would you like to spend more time outside during the day?
◇ Do you find areas of school too hectic, such as the playground or the corridor?

. . . .

. . . .

. . . .

. . . .

. . . .

. . . .

. . . .

. . . .

To help you design your perfect school, I suggest you get a large piece of plain paper and write on it three headings, 'Essential', 'Would be cool' and 'No way!' Or you could fill in the table. If you need more lines, ask someone to copy it for you. Feel free to add your own words.

ESSENTIAL	WOULD BE COOL	NO WAY!

Draw pictures if you want to, but make sure you put them under *one* of these three headings. Don't rush this. You are starting to find a solution to your difficult situation and it probably took more than 20 minutes to get to where you are now. *Take your time to complete this exercise.* It will help you focus on a school where you will be happy – either your current school or a new one. *It will be worth it taking some time on this.* Maybe do it over a couple of days, or a week or two?

Okay, when you've finished this exercise, start to think about (or reflect on) what changes you would like to see in your actual school. You can be as wild and creative as you like because your ideas will help the adults around you understand what you need.

Here are some things you might want to include in your 'ideal school':

Tangibles (things you can see, feel or measure):

◈ Size of the building
◈ Number of pupils who attend
◈ Subjects taught
◈ Size of playground
◈ Specialist school or mainstream school
◈ Specialist autism school
◈ Type of school – religious, science or dance specialism
◈ Teachers
◈ Headteacher
◈ Level of strictness
◈ Uniform rules
◈ Other school rules
◈ Canteen.

Your school might have children with different needs and abilities. Or it might be a grammar school, with lots of really clever children in it learning complicated things about maths, the sciences and technology. Everyone in your school might need to wear a uniform. Or you might be allowed to wear your own clothes, every single day! How many pupils in each lesson – 30? Or a lower number, like 15? Do you have the same teacher for all lessons, or do you have a new teacher for each subject? What do you prefer? Is there a music department? Is there space to cook in your school? Imagine you could build your own school, what would be in it? This is a fun activity, and an important way to create a vision for yourself. ☺

The point of all of this is to help you be clear about what would make school a happy place for you to be (even on your sad days). This is about listening to your voice and your ideas. Some of you will be on a shorter timetable or go to school on set days or part-days; it's good to explore lots of options, especially if being in school makes you feel overwhelmed. If it doesn't work for you, try to explain exactly why to your parent, who can then tell the school on your behalf.

Pixie explains the adjustments her school made to help her feel more comfortable:

> We started shortening the school day. The teacher wanted to know when I would be picked up from school in advance. I can see that was important from her perspective, but people could see how hard it was for me. I would stay for an hour or half an hour. I would go in and leave pretty much straight afterwards. Some days I would make it to lunch, but that meant I wasn't seeing my friends, which made everything a bit harder. It was a constant going in for an hour and five minutes on a bad day; sometimes I couldn't even leave the house, I did that for about a year, it was exhausting.

Like Pixie, you may find getting through the school day exhausting.

Here are some other suggestions you may wish to consider when thinking about how your current school could be improved, or a new school you might wish to go to.

Intangibles (things that are invisible, trickier to measure), things about school that can make it difficult for you to attend:

◇ Culture and ethos (ask an adult to explain what is meant by culture and ethos if you're not sure)
◇ Atmosphere
◇ Friendships

- ✧ Bullying
- ✧ Competition
- ✧ Self-esteem
- ✧ Not being believed
- ✧ Intense feelings and reactions
- ✧ Can't be yourself
- ✧ Feeling safe
- ✧ Nowhere to calm down or chill out
- ✧ Don't trust people.

Doing this exercise with Samila was fun. She provided clear examples of how she thought school could be improved for children with difference, either racial or having a different way of thinking and learning:

> I want change, so that future and current students can have the best possible experience at your school. Right from the beginning I want you to dedicate workshops weekly – ranging from different social issues and how to make school a better place – due to how workshops are more active and engaging than talks. I encourage a lot of these workshops to be around anti-racism, and acceptance to make society and school enjoyable for everyone. I would also recommend having mandatory reading for non-black students on anti-racism, mental health and for neurotypicals, too, about neurodivergence and how to be more accepting in general.

What sorts of things do you think are essential for a lovely school environment:

- ✧ Garden with flowers and trees?
- ✧ Nice food in the canteen?
- ✧ Therapy dog?
- ✧ Chill-out room?

Is there anything we've missed? What about your internal world...the world inside your head? Would you like to have a chill-out zone in your ideal school? Or yoga lessons?

When this activity is done it would be really helpful to you and the adults around you to do a similar activity creating a picture of your ideal day, in terms of how you would like to learn, what you would like to learn, what your teachers would be like, how many other children there would be in your class, what you would eat for lunch, where you would eat lunch, how long the lessons would be, and so on.

Your school environment

Now we're going to look at the school environment...which means all of the things that are external or *outside* of you that can influence how you feel. Funny thing is, every school is so different, even though you imagine all schools are pretty much the same!

There are usually lots of stairs. Lots of classrooms. A canteen or dining room. Some schools have a cloakroom, where all of the coats and bags are stored. Others have lockers. Lockers can be inside or outside of the school. Some schools have a library. A computer room. Tennis courts, a sports hall, a games room. Your school might have a sick bay or office where people go when they're feeling poorly. Most schools have a main hall, usually where they have assemblies, plays or parents' evenings. Some schools have thousands of pupils; others have a couple of hundred.

Life as a young adult

Children in more developed and wealthy countries are expected to go to school up to the age of either 16 or 18. Depending on the laws in the country where you live, you can legally increase the number of activities you can do outside of school, between the ages of 16 and 18. At 16 you can get married, or consent to sexual activity with other individuals who are also aged 16 or over. You can drink wine or beer with a meal if you're with someone who is over 18. You can get a National Insurance number. At 17 you can apply for a driving licence (in the UK), and worryingly, the police can interview you without an adult being present. You can register to vote. At 18 you can buy cigarettes, fireworks, place a bet, view pornographic material and get a tattoo.

Here are my tips to help you learn how to ADULT:

Ask lots of questions, ask different people. You might feel shy, but asking questions gives you the power to make an *informed decision* (with information).

Don't do anything that you don't want to; listen to that feeling inside. If something feels wrong or a bit 'off', *take time out before you act.* Take as long as you like.

Understand as much as you can about the decision you are making, and if you learn something you don't like, you can always say no.

Learn from your mistakes. You won't get everything right all of the time, but if something goes wrong, try to understand why it went wrong and remember it for next time.

Take responsibility for your decisions.

These activities can be life-changing and require a degree of personal maturity from you. But they're not compulsory – meaning *you don't have to do anything you don't want to, ever!* It's exciting to think of all the things you can do when you're an adult – there are so many choices. ☺ Some of these choices are difficult to understand and expensive and risky, so here's the thing – understanding how to be an adult and how to make good decisions isn't something that can be taught; you sort of learn as you go along.

Samila provides a great example of how she feels about herself and wants to be accepted:

> I like having blue hair as I feel it represents me in a way that breaks society's boundaries. I like how passionate I am about a wide range of topics. And I like how I have empathy. And I would like boys to be able to understand feminism and be more accepting of gender identity, sexism, racism, homophobia and ableism. I would like to see more punishments in schools for pupils who bully others because they are ignorant of these issues, or get a warning at least.
>
> The psychology behind this is that people discriminate because they think they can get away with it – however, if there are reputable and stable punishments, hopefully we can eliminate discrimination.

Alternative places and ways to learn

Now you've got some ideas about what would encourage you to return to school, by thinking in detail about your ideal school, you and the adults around you need to be realistic about what changes your current school is able to make. With your parent or teacher, you may agree that another school or type of school is the best option for you. Take your time before making any firm decisions.

- ✧ Give yourself time to recover from anything intense that happened at school that can create harmful associations about going to school.
- ✧ Take the opportunity to talk to someone about your personal feelings and how they get in the way of going to school.
- ✧ Try to understand your back-to-school plan. Try it out for a few weeks. Discuss what's working and what isn't with your chosen adults. Hopefully the adults around you will listen and be sensitive to your needs and support you, for as long as it takes, until you are happily re-settled back at school.
- ✧ Have you thought about home tuition? Or would you rather be with school friends? Can one of your parents be at home to support your home study or out-of-school learning activities, such as music, dance or other lessons?
- ✧ Some children have home tuition that's paid for by the local council, and I will talk you through this in Chapter 12 (see page 109).

A lot of stuff to cover, eh? I bet you never knew you had so many options, and that people really want to hear your opinions! Well done!

11

Being Away from the People and Places that Make You Feel Safe

In this chapter we will hear the voices of young people just like you. Listen out for their fab ideas and suggestions!

Pixie loved being at home. As she found school so noisy and stressful, her teacher came up with a brilliant idea to make her miss home a bit less:

I spent lots of time in the Resource Centre, out of the classroom completely, so by the end of the year, I was really good at typing, I was also helping with the juniors, they were, like, five years old! I LOVED it. There was one little girl who had Down's Syndrome, and we were such good friends. I would help her with her exercises. By the end I was like a teacher's assistant – I would help with photocopying, typing, I was like staff – hahaha. The rest of the school it was fine, but being in the classroom was hard.

I did feel guilty about not going to school, I was crying, and the teacher said, you see, this is what happens when you don't go to school! My friends would say 'can't you just **try** to get into school, we miss you'. My avoidance impacted all of our lives in quite big ways. People think if you're guilty enough you won't do it (stay off school), but it was the worst of both worlds; I felt guilty and still couldn't go into a classroom. If the pupils in my class were better behaved, maybe...if the teachers had just listened and believed me, that would have helped.

I can think of five kids in four weeks who are school avoiding. There are 300 kids in my school, in a small country, and we don't really talk about it! There are probably so many more. In Ireland, if the education welfare officer can see that you're trying, there are no penalties. And over here you can apply for 'home tuition', which is what I'm doing now; you can apply if you've got school anxiety. I have to have psychologist proof and from my parents, and the odds are I'm not going to get full hours next year.

(Note that home tuition is usually only granted for the most exceptional of cases.)

I asked Pixie to give her advice to kids like her:

I would advise other kids now that ***it's not your fault***. If I had a time machine and I could change any one of my actions, I realize that none of it was my fault. It's a hard thing to realize but it's also kind of therapeutic – none of this is your fault.

- ☐ Many of the reasons why you need to feel safe are based in your early childhood.
- ☐ You may have developed fears about being away from your key family members for a number of reasons.
- ☐ Due to cruel things and experiences as a younger child, you may have trauma.
- ☐ Learning difficulty and a neurodivergent condition can make being at home, with routines, very reassuring.
- ☐ Social anxiety, that is, fear talking to people, or thinking people won't like or accept you, especially new people.

When I chatted to Freddie (age 12), he had developed a dread of going to school, which stemmed from a traumatizing experience he had had with a little boy who had bullied him, an experience he hadn't got over yet:

There was one kid who always bullied me; when he came to my house, he tried to hurt my cat. I didn't tell mum or dad until later, I just kinda forgot to tell them. There were quite a few kids who picked on me, but he was the worst and it went on for years. I don't think the teachers realized it was that bad; he's moved away now, but I still think about it. I don't know how he did it; it still bothers me.

Nadia is 19 and is still upset by what happened to her when she was in primary school, way before she was diagnosed with autism:

My little friend group didn't really understand why I was skiving lessons. I didn't really explain to them I didn't know how to make friends. At secondary school the teachers were stricter and scarier but at the sixth form school the teachers were quite nice.

I found it so hard to make friends. I used to hide in the toilet in primary school, just to get away from everyone. Does that count as school avoidance? The anxiety is too much sometimes; my mum and dad didn't understand at all and used to try to drag me to school in the mornings. They got cross and I didn't want to go and I would miss the train – it was awful, but they didn't know. None of us knew. I got through primary school, but it all started to go wrong at secondary school. I just couldn't cope at all and went to school, then would need a day off to recover. I did make some friends, but they didn't really understand.

I asked Nadia what would have helped:

My advice to other young people – I'm different, other people have people who like them; I felt I couldn't get better, but I did! What would help me (at school) is precise, clear instructions. Sometimes if I ask for help, should I do this, and they (the teachers) say it's up to you!

Because I'm so confident, and I can talk and answer questions, during lessons they will think there's nothing wrong with me. I hope my contribution helps and maybe could help a wider school system! [She gives a thumbs-up.]

How do you feel hearing the other young people's stories?

. . . .

. . . .

The Magic Question

IF YOU COULD CHANGE ONE THING IN
YOUR LIFE, WHAT WOULD IT BE?

In this chapter, we're going to leave the real world behind for a while and delve into our imaginations. This is a bit like when you are asked to write stories at school, and your English teacher tells you to make something up. It's usually at this point that your mind goes completely blank! You think your teacher has gone completely mad – how on earth are you supposed to make something up out of thin air?

The funny thing is that your imagination is like a fire that's always burning in a low crackle. If you've ever been camping and someone throws something on the fire, it goes up in a fast whoosh and burns really brightly for a few minutes until it dies down again! Your imagination is like that campfire – you need to keep throwing logs on it to keep it burning. Can you guess what those logs are made of? They are your ideas, wishes, fears and experiences. Whenever you feel low or unsure of something, try throwing your ideas, fears and wishes into the fire of your imagination. You will be amazed by how much power this gives you. Your mind will start to take over and you will be able to start to figure things out, especially if you really focus on what you want. And as an added bonus, this skill will help you to write fantastic stories that will amaze your teacher.

Do you like making up stories? If you do, you're going to enjoy this chapter. If you're not too keen on writing stories, you can still have fun by making them up in your head – you don't even need to write them down! You can make up whatever silly thing you want. Such as...a crazy tale about a talking blob of lime-green jelly that really *hates* ice cream and decides to turn into a lump of rock every time someone puts ice cream next to it! Clever, huh? This is the jelly's way of saying they're not happy about something. Or you could make up a story about a sad little boy who turns into a dragon when he's angry and flames come out of his mouth when he's upset. Or a story about a child who has an invisible friend she tells all her secrets to...

Finding our personal Imagination Land is the opposite of being in Real Life – IRL. Let's call it IIL (in Imagination Land). There are a few things to remember:

◇ If you are as quiet and calm as possible, it's much easier to get into Imagination Land.
◇ It works best when you are away from any screens, such as phones or computers, as they interfere with the imagination brainwaves.
◇ Close your eyes and breathe slowly in and out three times. This helps to calm your body and your mind.

Using your imagination is like having a superpower. You are in control, and no one has the magic wand apart from you. Imagine that for a minute – you can use your imaginary wand to make or create anything you want in the world! Sounds great, doesn't it? You can also use your imaginary wand to make bad or sad things disappear – that's even cooler! Do you feel ready to step into Imagination Land? Okay. After a count of three, slowly close your eyes and take a deep breath in, 1–2–3, and now take a deep breath out, 3–2–1!

And repeat. Don't worry if you feel worried or frightened when you close your eyes; maybe you can ask someone you trust to sit with you. When you've done this deep breathing two more times, you will feel calm enough to start to think about things that you don't usually think about. Open your eyes after the third time. When you open your eyes, everything may look the same around you, but while you were calming yourself, with your eyes closed, your brain was relaxing and calming down too. Now blow the air out of your mouth slowly so it makes an 'ooooooohhhhhh' sound, like you are blowing out candles on your birthday cake. Then say in a strong, clear voice:

> I'm in Imagination Land; it's safe and exciting here. I can create ANYTHING I want!

> I can make things disappear. I can make things appear. I can think and talk about my fears, worries and my dreams and wishes.

> Only I have the power to do this, this is My Special Place.

The weird thing about being in Imagination Land is that it might look exactly like your bedroom or your kitchen or wherever it was you started, but it's designed that way to make you feel safe. The signals in your brain that usually fizz around when you feel stressed, anxious or upset are dampened down when you breathe deeply.

In fact, it's a great idea to take a few deep breaths whenever you feel stressed, as it can actually help your whole body to calm down. It's so powerful, that if you practise deep breathing regularly, you will start to feel more chilled and confident in yourself and you will be less likely to flip out over small things. Sounds good, huh? So why doesn't everyone do it? The truth is, 'breathwork' is quite popular with adults, especially those who are into yoga. But lots of kids your age find it more difficult to calm busy minds, which is understandable, as young people have lots of difficult things going on in life.

If you find it hard to sit still and breathe, try standing up and stretching your arms in the air as high as they can go. Breathe in when you put your arms up and breathe out again when you put them down. This also works well. Do whatever it takes to make you feel calm and steady and ready to explore your thoughts and feelings.

So, are you ready to take a dive into your imagination with me?

WOW – you've done it – now let's get to work...

If you could change *one* thing in your life, what would it be? Okay. Write that word on some paper or ask someone to write it for you.

Once you have this ONE THING in your life, think of *three* words to describe how you would feel.

In this new world, what else would change? Write a story about your new world. (Remember, you are in Imagination Land, so it can be anything wild, fantastic and something you thought would never be true. *This is your world; you are in control of everything...*)

If you prefer to draw a picture, grab some pens, paper and glue, and create a new world where you'd like to live. Remember to use all of your feelings in this world, good or bad. Show your picture to someone you trust, and tell them all about it and how it works.

What makes the magic question special? Any ideas? Try gazing into an imaginary fire and see where your mind takes you.

Ignite the fire of your imagination

Yes – it's free!

Yes – it's easy to do!

Yes – it makes you feel better!

YES. And the really special thing is that it works. Thinking about how you'd like life to change right now is really exciting, once you get past feeling scared. And feeling fearful is natural. We might be human beings, but we are still animals. Fear is a strong and ancient part of human development that helps to keep us safe. Centuries ago, when wild animals roamed the earth, it was important for humans to have a fast-acting signal of any danger – ignoring danger could mean the difference between life and death! Our brain developed a super-fast warning system in the brain – like an alarm system – which means that when we think we're in danger, our bodies get ready to react.

I hope you enjoyed being in Imagination Land. Take a few moments to come back into this reality and get used to your surroundings.

Using this technique of taking yourself off somewhere helps you in two ways – relaxing your mind and also beginning to problem-solve. Each time you do this, it gets easier.

Not going to school: sounds *amazing*, right?! Every single school is different. A school can have thousands of variations, and while you may be fortunate to get a 'free' education, that doesn't mean you will enjoy the experience of the school where you are now.

Read these questions carefully and think about some of the ones that relate to you. To help you complete this challenge, I've broken it down into sections:

Schoolwork:

- ✧ What subjects do you love?
- ✧ What are you good at?
- ✧ What do you need help with?
- ✧ What do you hate?
- ✧ What would you love to learn about that you're not learning at the moment?

Teachers:

- ✧ Are there some teachers who are patient with you?
- ✧ Do you feel embarrassed or ashamed in their lesson?
- ✧ Do the teachers know you feel this way?

✧ Do teachers listen to your concerns and answer your questions?
✧ Do you tell teachers when you don't understand something?
✧ Do you feel some teachers are too strict?
✧ Do you think some teachers are impatient?
✧ Are there some teachers who are kind and patient?
✧ Is there at least one teacher you can talk to, either about your personal worries or your school worries?

Socials:

✧ Do you have many friends?
✧ Would you like to make lots of friends or just a few who 'get' you?
✧ Do you talk to any of your school friends about your worries and concerns?
✧ Do you think any of your friends have similar issues to you?
✧ Do you keep secrets from your friends?
✧ Do you think other people don't like you?
✧ Who do you talk to who is your own age?
✧ Do you have friends you talk to online?
✧ Do you share information about yourself with your online friends?
✧ Do you overshare in groups and regret it afterwards?
✧ Do you feel unsafe online sometimes?
✧ Is there someone you talk to about this, or do you use any other online service for young people?
✧ Do you find it hard to slot into a conversation?
✧ Do you feel physical sensations of nervousness when you're with other people? (e.g., clammy hands, heart racing, shaky voice.)

Personals:

✧ Do you feel confident in your own skin?
✧ Are there parts of you that you would like to change?

✧ Do you feel unsure about your sexuality?

✧ Are you concerned about any of your bodily changes (especially the growth towards adulthood)?

✧ Are their changes to your body that worry you?

✧ Do you know who to talk to about these?

✧ Do you find personal hygiene difficult (e.g., brushing teeth, showering, hair washing)?

Big feelings:

✧ Do you get angry easily?

✧ Do you cry a lot?

✧ Do you bottle up your big feelings?

✧ Do you sometimes feel you can't be bothered to do anything – even getting up is a struggle?

✧ Do your feelings make you feel exhausted?

Culture:

✧ Do you speak a different language at home to at school?

◇ Is your culture unusual in your school community?

✧ Do you feel like you stand out too much?

✧ Do people see your culture as dangerous, strange or aggressive?

✧ Do wish you were invisible?

✧ 'I don't belong here/at school/in this country/in this community' – do you agree with this statement?

✧ Do you wear different clothes in your community for cultural or religious reasons (e.g., hijab, headscarf, long skirts, cover face, don't cut hair)?

✧ Are you comfortable doing this?

As you read this workbook you will start to understand that there are things you don't like, things that make you feel happy, and things and people that really annoy you. This is all fine. Everyone is unique and has a cluster of things that they are naturally good at with groups of people they enjoy being with and certain things that help them feel calm.

Take a few minutes to think about the things, places or people who are in your 'tribe'. And think of ONE thing that makes you feel at peace and content:

. . . .

ONE place that makes you feel like yourself:

. . . .

ONE thing that calms you down:

. . . .

ONE person who makes you feel good about yourself and likes you for who you are, even when you feel grumpy:

. . . .

When you talk to your parent or adult support person, share your thoughts about these four things as it will help them to understand you and some of the barriers that may be getting in the way of you going to school. This is important because learning in a school building with lots of other young people, doing lessons you either don't like or find hard to understand, with students or teachers who don't get you – it's tough. A big change might be necessary for you to feel safe, well and continue to learn.

But what if you don't want to go to school anymore?

This is tricky. The longer you are absent from school, the more stress you may build up about going back to school. And the more stress you build up inside, the harder it is to even think about facing everyone: your teacher, your friends, your frenemies.

It feels like a big weight on your shoulders, and here's the really funny thing. Although you feel pretty grown up and 'on it' a lot of the time, sometimes there is too much to think about and you just want to be cuddled.

Here are six top tips to break through your overwhelm:

1. Be kind to yourself.
2. Break your big problem into lots of smaller ones.
3. Tackle one problem a day.
4. Only move on to the next problem once you are happy that you have dealt with the first one.
5. And repeat. Make sure in all of your discussions that your voice is heard. Even if you are under the age of 16, it's important that you have your say on your future.
6. If there is a team of adults around you, ask for their help. You don't need to make any decisions by yourself. Write any questions in the space below, so you won't forget them when it's your time to meet with the teachers.

My questions for the teachers:

. . . .

. . . .

Important note: There is an organization called the United Nations and they have created a document, a Convention, that outlines the rights of the child, which explains how they protect children around the world. The key message of this Convention is: every child has rights, whatever their ethnicity, gender, religion, language, abilities or any other status. It's comforting to know that there are laws in place to protect children just like you.

Alternative places to learn

There are a number of things that may be outside of your control, which your parents or other support adults will need to take care of, things like travel to school, special therapies or counselling. There are *always* options regarding your schooling or alternative places for you to learn. In the UK, learning in other places that are not school is shortened to EOTAS (education otherwise than at school). EOTAS is an alternative provision (AP), which sometimes means another school or even another learning environment completely.

EOTAS is a formal legal arrangement that explains that a young person with an EHC (Education, Health and Care) plan can receive special educational support even if they are unable to attend school. This means that in some circumstances, you could study in a place that's not a registered educational setting, such as a library or community centre. The key thing to remember is that EOTAS is agreed on if it is *inappropriate* for you to be educated in school. This is why it's important for you to be honest and have your say, if you don't want decisions that affect you to be made for you. It's also important that you have given the 'learning at school' plan your 100% commitment before you feel that you need to try something else.

If you are going down the EOTAS road, consider the following:

✧ You may be lonely, as you won't have your friends with you every day.
✧ If your teacher is a parent, that can get a bit intense.
✧ Does/Do the adult(s) teaching you know enough about all of the subjects you like, e.g., music, PE, drama, art etc.?
✧ It may be difficult to stick to a routine without the structure of school.
✧ You will miss out on whole-school activities such as trips to museums, theatre visits, foreign trips, sporting fixtures etc.

If your family has opted for you to learn at home, this is called EHE (elective home education). None of this is stuff you need to worry about; this is more of the legal stuff your parents need to be aware of. The key thing is that you're learning, growing in confidence and have good daily wellbeing practice. AP places of learning can be really enjoyable and fun places to be.

A special sort of AP is called a Pupil Referral Unit (PRU). This is where you are transferred to if your existing school isn't able to meet your needs. For some young people a PRU offers the *flexibility and freedom from the daily stress* of lessons and teachers. It might be the right choice for you. Some pupils have all of their lessons in a PRU;

others will split their time between their usual school and the PRU. Every situation is different.

Although this can be a worrying time for you, it's important to remember three things:

1. People are trying to help you.
2. School and learning is important, and so is your health and wellness.
3. You learn better when you feel better.

Generally, if you attend a PRU, you are likely to need more care and support than your current school can provide. If you attend this sort of school, you may be waiting for a diagnosis to work out exactly what sort of care you need. If you've recently had an autism diagnosis, for example, it's important for you to work out what it means for YOU – not just in terms of school and learning, but also what it means for you as an individual.

Other young people can find these places of learning too unstructured, with a mix of young people who have different needs, including autism, ADHD, behavioural or mental ill health difficulties or short-term illness. This means that while the environment works for you, coping with the emotions of the other children and young people can be difficult. It's important that you visit the PRU and talk about the options if you feel unable to return to your current school.

Each place is different, so try to make sure you have a chance to see them all yourself and ask questions – as many as you can – before you agree to go. I know it's hard as a young person, because lots of adults think they know what's best for you. If they say you will like this school, or this will be good for you, just ask, why? Or say 'Please explain'. It's not being rude or argumentative, but remember:

◇ Adults can feel as stressed as you about making the right decision.
◇ They might be your parent, but they don't really understand you.

◇ Try to ask questions when you feel calm, and when you think the adults around you are calm.
◇ Write down your questions, if possible.
◇ If you have a big worry about something about the new school, don't be afraid to speak up. Speaking up now may save a lot of pain and stress later on if you have to change schools again.

Reduced timetable

A reduced timetable means you remain on the register or 'roll' of your school, and you need to go into school for certain lessons or subjects. The times and dates that you go to school will be agreed between the school and your main parent and usually yourself. This sort of planning is often most successful if your thoughts are at the centre of the decision-making. Your reduced timetable will be in place, and once it's started it will stay the same unless the school think you are able to manage more hours in school and in more lessons. You should have your say in this, too.

Home education or 'home school'

This is a big area and means different things to different families. In its simple form, it means that the bulk of your learning is done away from a school building, and your parents will understand what you learn and how. You may work mostly from home, but your learning may be freer in style than school.

Years ago, home-schooled young people would be teased for being different. In the last 10 years or more, parents have realized that home-educated young people are gaining top qualifications, university degrees, or are successful entrepreneurs, and, most importantly, many find great peace and happiness as a result of their unique education. They appreciate that they were free from bullying, worries about uniforms, social pressure – that they were free from doing things they didn't want to.

Pixie describes her home-schooling experience after being out of school for more than two years:

I have three teachers – they come to the house, I do six subjects a week and rotate science and maths because there aren't enough hours to do them every week. I love being home schooled; I've always loved learning and I haven't been getting a proper education for years! I love that I'm finally back learning on a regular basis; the drawback is that most of the classes are in the afternoon, so I feel a bit isolated in the mornings, as most of my friends are in school when I'm at home and out in the afternoon, but when my dad's not working, we go and visit my aunties and uncles and grandparents or go to the cinema, or me and my mum will go the shops. And I'm starting volunteering for the Red Cross. It's a great scheme, but you're only given the hours if they can see that you're making an effort to come back into schooling. As much as a I enjoy the home school, it's overshadowed by the fact that I have to prove that I'm traumatized enough to get the hours, and what I went through was big enough that I need this.

Forest school, wild or outdoors learning or self-directed learning

Forest school or wild or outdoors learning is becoming more popular as large numbers of children are unable to manage in mainstream schools. The forest school movement is a child-centred learning and educational environment with a predominantly outdoors learning setting. Depending on the learning model, the content can be environmentally focused, or include elements of the scientific and creative curriculum, using nature as the backdrop. Many of its proponents speak of the simultaneously calming and invigorating aspects of learning outdoors, which provides sensory-stimulating and sensory-soothing elements, which can be particularly helpful for neurodivergent learners.

Another form of learning that may interest you is self-directed learning, which is basically learning without teachers and outside of a formal learning environment. This type of learning suits young people who are highly motivated to learn about a particular subject, so this may suit some autistic youngsters who wish to delve deeply into a specialist subject, and be free to learn in their own time in their own way.

There is a lot to think about in this chapter. Do you feel a bit more excited about learning, now you know there are so many options as well as learning at school? If you can get through school, you are free to follow your own dreams to what you want to do, although you may need to have achieved some basic educational stepping-stones first.

Don't give up hope!

The Word Wall

Building a Word Wall with a group of people your age is a great way to work through your feelings. It's also helpful to know that other people your age feel the same way about things that you do. If you want to talk to an adult about your big feelings but don't know where to start, this is a great idea.

You don't need a group to do this exercise – just two people can do this together. The main thing to remember is that you are both honest about the words you write down. Don't worry about the spellings or whether your writing is neat – the main thing is just to write the words down.

If you've never used a Word Wall, now is the time to start – it's such fun. Let me explain. A Word Wall is a visual place to dump all of the main words that relate to a particular topic, and it usually relates to your inner world. For example, I did a Word Wall with a group of young people (aged between 12 and 13) at a drama workshop to help them come to terms with their experiences of lockdown during the outbreak of COVID-19. I asked them to think about their challenges and what was difficult for them, and for them to fill a piece of paper with their emotion words. Because there were seven children, we stuck several pieces of A3 paper together to make a 'giant' Word Wall, with plenty of space for everyone to write their words.

When everyone who is doing the Word Wall has finished writing all of the words that were in their head, sit back and look at all of those big emotions on the paper. Afterwards you each take turns in saying the following:

Thank you for sharing your feelings honestly.

These are really powerful words – this must have been a strong experience for you.

Is there anything else you feel about this that you haven't written on the paper?

How do you feel now that you've done this?

Here are some of the words that filled the Word Wall:

- ♦ Scared
- ♦ Not seeing friends
- ♦ Hidden
- ♦ Anxious
- ♦ Worried
- ♦ Inside.

Emotional state

- ♦ Change in behaviour
- ♦ Motivational aspect
- ♦ Physiological change
- ♦ Provoked by our environment.

If you're a young person with ADHD, your emotions may come up quickly and fiercely, and it can be hard to control these feelings. Don't worry – this is partly due to your condition, and partly due to it not being properly managed, which causes you to have a short fuse. Doing this word exercise will help you 'name' some of the strong emotions so people can understand you better. Naming emotions, either on paper or using your voice to share what you are feeling with other people, is enormously helpful. Especially when the words going round in your head can make you feel exhausted and sadder. However you do it, it's good to get the words out of your brain! When you start you may find that the words just flow.

> Do you feel relief that the words belonging to those strong emotions are no longer in your head?

> We can start to say goodbye to those feelings about that particular thing from this moment.

> I can see it was a difficult time for you.

> It seems that we shared a lot of the same feelings.

Ask your trusted adult to print off a picture of planet Earth and write or draw as many positive words or images as you can about what you think the world should be like – be creative! Colour this in and put it on your bedroom wall. ☺

Here's an idea: Going to school will help you get the education you need to make some of these changes in the world that you want to see.

The Pleasures and Pains of Being YOU, Including Self-Care

This chapter is probably THE most important one in the whole workbook. I suggest you read this one as often as you can! Get into it daily, especially when lots of things seem to be going wrong. This chapter can make you feel better and *fast*.

Look after your body

You may have heard about the need to boost your *immunity* to keep yourself well and ensure that if you do come into contact with COVID-19, or any other illness or virus for that matter, that your body is strong enough to fight it off quickly. We've talked a lot about stress in this workbook and I want you to understand that prolonged stress is unhealthy for the body. You build up a stack of stress hormones that damage your ability to heal and fight infections. Read Chapter 8 again to refresh your memory on tips to keep your stress levels low.

Eat well

This sounds obvious, but it really is important. This is a good time to reduce sugar and ditch the processed and junk food. Try different tastes or eat the rainbow![1]

---

1   This means eating foods from all of the food groups in lots of different colours, which can be visually stimulating as well as healthy, and encourages a varied diet.

Sleep

Give yourself the best chance of sleep. It's equally as important as food, but often forgotten. Give yourself a big sleep window. If you set aside 10 hours, you'll get your 7 or 8. If you set aside 7, you'll get less than you need.

Reduce stress

As with all external events, it is our response that dictates whether we get stressed, not the event itself. Try the following:

- ◇ *Meditate* morning and evening to bracket the day with some much-needed stillness.
- ◇ *Move:* Do some gentle yoga and stretch your body or get out for a walk or run in fresh air as often as you can.

Shifting negative thoughts into positive thoughts

Try letting things go. If you've heard of the word 'Zen', you will know what this final chapter is all about. It's about accepting what is, knowing the difference between what you can change and what you can't, practising feeling calm about what happens, even when things don't always go to plan.

One of the best ways to do this is to: *spend some time each evening planning for the next day.* Make a written list of things that need to be accomplished. These are called goals. Like in football, you want to get the ball into the net – it's a very clear goal. You may have a clear goal to do some revision, or practise your dance routine, or get an early night. So you practise it, and then you do it. The ball either goes in the net or it doesn't. And if it doesn't, what do you do? Try again and keep practising.

Draw up a game plan for each item on your list. That way, you're not thinking of new things after you go to bed and staying awake worrying about them.

It is scientifically proven that if you write stuff down you are:

◇ More likely to do it, or
◇ More likely to achieve a goal you have set for yourself.

A goal doesn't need to be big or fancy-schmanzy – it could be as simple as getting out of bed before 10am and have something to eat before 11am. Or reading 10 pages of this workbook and chatting to your mum, dad or therapist about it.

Accepting you have done your best, planned and prepared gives you some confidence. And you can be kind to yourself knowing that you did your bit, but you can't plan everything. Sometimes life throws you 'curveballs', which means that they don't end up where they were expected to. This happens to everyone.

Here are some other things you can do to slide your brain into a happier, coping state:

◇ *Write down three things* you like about yourself and three things other people like about you. (Ask someone else to help you write these.)
◇ *Meditate* – there are some amazing guided meditations online.
◇ *Happy activity* – spend regular time on your happy activity (the clue is in the word, it needs to be a physical activity). This is because moving your body releases happy hormones.
◇ *Start a private journal* with pictures, stickers, thoughts and memories. When good things happen, you need to write them down, so when your pesky negative anxiety mind springs up, you have some lovely memories to counterbalance it. GO you!

GOOD NEWS: You have some excellent tools to use when you have problems with people or things are not working out. If one idea doesn't work, you have other ideas to try.

Thank you for working so hard on your relationship with school and what's happening there and on your mental wellbeing. I'm sure you will start to grow into the wonderful person you are becoming. Well done – I'm super-proud that you've stuck with this process.

Online Help and Resources

If you live in the UK, the youth suicide charity Papyrus runs a helpline for young people called HOPELINEUK. They provide confidential support and advice and can be contacted on 0800 068 4141, you can also text 07860039967 or email pat@papyrus-uk.org, and in the UK and Ireland, the Samaritans can be contacted on 116 123, or email jo@samaritans.org or jo@samaritans.ie.

If you're in the United States, the National Suicide Prevention Lifeline is on 800 273 8255. You can also text HOME to 741741 to connect with a crisis text line counsellor.

Here are some websites you can visit to explore issues in more detail if you wish. It's always a good idea to talk to someone about your problems. Finding out a bit more online is useful too. Try to talk to an adult you trust about your difficulties, especially if you need to go to any appointments. It's usually best to be honest about what's happening. Luckily for most children, family members and trusted adults are usually happy that you talked to them and are ready to help in any way they can.

One more thing: you should *never* go to anyone's house or go to any appointments on your own. When you go out anywhere, always let someone know exactly where you are going and leave some contact details. However difficult things might be for you, it is always important to stay safe. ☺

Beat Eating Disorders: www.beateatingdisorders.org.uk

THE SCHOOL NON-ATTENDER'S WORKBOOK

Better Health, Every Mind Matters, National Health Service (NHS): www.nhs.uk/every-mind-matters

Childline, general information, advice and support: 0800 1111, www.childline.org.uk

FRANK, for honest information about drugs: www.talktofrank.com

Hope Again, living after loss and bereavement, stories from young people suffering from loss: www.hopeagain.org.uk

Kooth, your online wellbeing community: www.kooth.com

No More Panic, provides members with support and advice if they have anxiety, phobias and obsessive-compulsive disorder (OCD), and you could make friends along the way: www.nomorepanic.co.uk

OCD-UK provide advice, information and support for those with OCD: www.ocduk.org

Students Against Depression: www.studentsagainstdepression.org

The HIS Project, happyinschool – autism, ADHD education and advocacy, supporting you in school if you have a diagnosis of autism or ADHD: www.happyinschoolproject.com

Young Minds, mental health issues: www.youngminds.org.uk

Young Minds, your feelings: www.youngminds.org.uk/young-person/my-feelings

Blank for Notes

....

....

....

....

....

....

....

....

....

....

....

....

....

....

....

....

....

....

....

....

....

....

....

....

....

....

....

....

....

....

....

....

....

....

....

....

....